Musical Futures

An approach
to teaching
and learning

RESOURCE PACK: 2ND EDITION

Compiled and edited by
Abigail D'Amore

musical futures

paul hamlyn foundation
special project

musical futures

paul hamlyn foundation
special project

phf Paul Hamlyn
Foundation

Paul Hamlyn Foundation
18 Queen Anne's Gate
London SW1H 9AA

ISBN: 978-1-905500-19-2

Cover image: Rubberball/Getty Images
Inside images: Emile Holba (www.emileholba.co.uk)

Mixed Sources
Product group from well-managed
forests and other controlled sources
www.fsc.org Cert no. SGS-COC-004224
FSC © 1996 Forest Stewardship Council

Designed by COG

Musical Futures
An approach to teaching and learning
RESOURCE PACK: 2ND EDITION

Foreword

I'm delighted to be able to introduce this second edition of the Musical Futures resource pack. As a former teacher myself, I'm very aware of the pressures that come with the job and of the need to be able to get hold of high-quality materials for use in the classroom.

I've always been passionate about music and its life-changing capacity. As an aspiring musician I was lucky enough to experience the thrill and immediacy of playing in bands. Whilst I understand the importance of absorbing the nuts and bolts of music theory, and of playing under direction, there are few things as spontaneously creative as a bunch of friends, a set of instruments, and seeing where the music takes you. Most professional musicians take this daily miracle for granted, but for the majority of young people it's a mysterious 'gift'.

It seems to me that these resources – many of which echo the way I learned to play informally – are about making those kinds of experiences available to all young people in school. They may not go on to become professional musicians but they'll begin to understand music from the inside out and perhaps transfer the confidence they gain from working in groups to other aspects of their learning, and indeed their lives.

The success of Musical Futures shows that music teachers are willing to try unconventional approaches and put themselves in situations where they don't always feel comfortable, if it means that their students make more music, more often. I'm thrilled to be able to support this project, and I hope more music teachers will feel sufficiently inspired by these resources to give them a try in their schools.

Sting
PATRON, MUSICAL FUTURES

SECTION 1
Introduction

Musical Futures
An approach to teaching and learning

RESOURCE PACK: 2ND EDITION

Welcome to the second edition of the Musical Futures resource materials. Since July 2006 when the official pathfinder work finished, Musical Futures has transformed from a pilot project into an approach to teaching and learning that is now recognised as a major initiative in secondary music education.

The first edition of the resource materials enabled teachers, practitioners and others to take the models and ideas developed by the pathfinders, and to adapt, adopt, refine, develop and personalise them in their own teaching or other educational situations. This started a process whereby teachers/practitioners try Musical Futures, overcome challenges, witness benefits and impact on students, and then become natural advocates for the approach and ultimately support others. In turn, this led to a real need for Continuing Professional Development, networking and opportunities to share good practice, which we responded to in the first instance through a national CPD training programme and subsequently via our Champion Schools initiative. We now estimate that more than 1000 secondary schools are running Musical Futures (which has increased from 60 during the pathfinder years), as well as the approaches being embedded into Music Service, Local Authority and Initial Teacher Training policy, and adapted by overseas colleagues.

Therefore, this pack is more than a second edition. It is a culmination of years of work, feedback and ideas from those who have tried Musical Futures and have openly and honestly shared what works and what doesn't. It also pays tribute to the project managers, teachers, music educators, academics, and perhaps most importantly the young people, who were involved in the pathfinder programmes of Musical Futures for developing ideas and models that could so successfully be replicated.

These resource materials do not have one author – they represent the work of many people, and we hope that resources will continue to be developed by teachers, practitioners and others who join Musical Futures.

I sincerely hope that you find this second edition useful, and adaptable to suit your needs and those of your students. Musical Futures survives because of the innovation and inspirational work of those who take it on.

Abigail D'Amore

Abigail D'Amore
MUSICAL FUTURES NATIONAL COORDINATOR

○ AN INTRODUCTION TO MUSICAL FUTURES

Musical Futures is an approach to teaching and learning. It is a new way of thinking about music-making in schools that brings non-formal teaching and informal learning approaches into the more formal context of schools.

Through Musical Futures, we frequently make use of the terms formal, non-formal and informal. The definitions we have given to these are:

FORMAL	Taught by adults in schools, colleges, etc
NON-FORMAL	Led by adults in community contexts
INFORMAL	Led by young people: • Working alone without the constant presence of adults • Students as teachers/teachers as students • No entry barriers to learning

We believe music learning works best when young people are making music

Musical Futures is not a scheme of work. It is a series of models and approaches that can be personalised by teachers, practitioners and others. It is based on the belief that music learning is most effective when young people are engaged in making music, and when their existing passion for music is acknowledged, reflected on and built-upon in the classroom.

At its heart is a commitment to:

○ Find ways of engaging all young people in the 11–18 age range in meaningful, sustainable musical activities

○ Make music learning relevant to young people, and connecting their in-school and out-of-school interests and experiences

○ Enable young people to experience practical music making, to understand the processes of music making, and for music making to contribute to their overall social, educational and personal development

This tends to happen in Musical Futures by:

○ Students working through a variety of non-formal and informal teaching and learning styles, ensuring that their individual learning needs are met

○ Valuing students' personal musical interests

○ Motivating students first, before moving them into other musical and learning styles

○ Making use of aural learning, that fully integrates listening with practical music making, improvising and composing

○ Teachers and practitioners flexing their teaching and learning styles to act as facilitators and through showing rather than telling, guiding and modelling rather than instructing

○ Students acting as peer leaders

○ Technique, notation and other forms of written instruction being part of the process, but rarely the starting point

INTRODUCTION

◉ BACKGROUND

The Musical Futures journey began in 2003 when the Paul Hamlyn Foundation, an independent grant-making foundation, instigated an initiative to find new and imaginative ways of engaging all young people, aged 11–18, in meaningful music activities. The starting point for Musical Futures was to understand the factors affecting the apparent disengagement of young people with sustained music-making activities, at a time in their lives when music is not only a passion for many young people, but plays a big part in shaping their social identity.

A year of consultation was followed by two years of 'Pathfinder' action research projects, where teams in Leeds, Nottingham and Hertfordshire trialled a number of learning models to find ways of engaging all young people in music-making, both in and out of school. The pathfinders were Music Services working in partnership with young people, schools, universities, professional music organisations and community music organisations. Alongside this, a number of research and development projects were also commissioned.

Following the development of tried-and-tested models, the first set of teacher resource materials were published in 2006 and made available free of charge.

The following provides a brief outline of the pathfinders, research and development partners, and where to find further information.

FURTHER READING
A series of pamphlets outlining the philosophy and development of Musical Futures are available for free download from **www.musicalfutures.org.uk/c/pamphlets**

TEACHER RESOURCE MATERIALS
These materials are still available to download from **www.musicalfutures.org.uk/c/first+edition**

PATHFINDERS, RESEARCH AND DEVELOPMENT PARTNERS

	Brief description of project	Age range of pupils designed for	Reference
Hertfordshire pathfinder	Hertfordshire Music Service in partnership with the Institute of Education, University of London piloted a programme of informal learning, developed by Professor Lucy Green (Institute of Education) and drawing on the real-life learning practices of popular musicians.	Years 8/9	*Classroom Resources for Informal Music Learning* available from **www.musicalfutures.org.uk/c/first+edition**
Nottingham pathfinder	Nottingham City Music Service piloted a *Whole Curriculum Approach* that aimed to develop school music beyond classroom confines, and involve students in real musical activity, in genuine musical situations and environments. It aimed to draw together good practice from classroom, instrumental and extra-curricular music into an integrated package for students.	Year 8	*Whole Curriculum Approach* available from **www.musicalfutures.org.uk/c/first+edition**
Leeds pathfinder	Education Leeds Artforms developed an approach to extra-curricular learning to empower young people to make positive, informed choices about the music they engage with beyond the classroom.	11–18 year olds	*Personalising Extra-Curricular Music for 11–18 Year Olds* available from **www.musicalfutures.org.uk/extra+curricular+provision**
Synergy.tv	Synergy.tv created a learning space for young people to publish their music.	All	**www.numu.org.uk**
Sound Connections	The 'Musical Routes' advice, information and guidance service created by Sound Connections (London Youth Music Action Zone) enabled young people in London to have more control over their learning pathways.	All	**www.musicalroutes.co.uk**
Guildhall CONNECT	A case study by Peter Renshaw of the Guildhall School of Music and Drama's CONNECT programme was commissioned to identify key elements of non-formal music making.	All	*Transforming Musical Leadership; Simply CONNECT* (Peter Renshaw) available from **www.musicalfutures.org.uk/c/pamphlets**
ICT	The report 'Electrifying Music' by David Ashworth was commissioned to support teachers and music leaders with using technology in their work with young people.	All	Available from **www.musicalfutures.org.uk/electrifying+music**

◐ WHO IS MUSICAL FUTURES FOR?

Musical Futures was initially designed for secondary schools, with a particular focus on 11–14 year old students (Key Stage 3), as this has traditionally been an age when students can lose interest in music learning in school.

It is also the point at which *all* students receive a music education entitlement, before they elect to continue (or not) during Key Stage 4. Teachers in primary and tertiary education have also successfully adopted Musical Futures approaches – certainly the synergies with Wider Opportunities in the primary sector are leading schools to look at hybrid Wider Opportunities/Musical Futures programmes that cross the transition divide (see page 76 for an example of this). Musical Futures has also been tailored for use with students in challenging circumstances, for example students with special educational needs, or in Young Offenders Institutes and Pupil Referral Units.

◐ CHAMPION SCHOOLS AND TRAINING

Even though the majority of teachers and practitioners establish and run Musical Futures using only the resource materials, there is an ongoing need for Continuing Professional Development surrounding Musical Futures practice – to share ideas, debate issues, and develop new resources and projects that can be used in the classroom.

In 2008, Musical Futures launched its 'Champion Schools' programme in partnership with Roland UK (**www.roland.co.uk**). Schools from around England who had adapted and adopted Musical Futures successfully were invited to apply to become Champion Schools, and to devise and run training and CPD for other teachers and practitioners in their region, funded by the Paul Hamlyn Foundation. Roland supported this by providing the selected Champion Schools with high quality equipment and technology for their training programmes and also to support their Musical Futures classroom work.

As a result, free-of-charge Musical Futures training and CPD days are now operational nationally, and attract delegates from across the music education sector. The training and CPD days are practical, hands-on, and usually involve students either through lesson observations or as coaches in the delivery of the practical work. The Champion Schools present Musical Futures in the way that they have developed it, meaning that delegates get a realistic insight into how Musical Futures can be adapted in a school environment.

There is an ongoing need for Continuing Professional Development surrounding Musical Futures practice

▶ RESULTS

Musical Futures engages all students in music participation

Recent independent research indicates that Musical Futures:

- Increases student motivation for, and enjoyment of, school music
- Engages all students in music participation
- Helps students to become more confident with music making and raises self-esteem
- Engages previously disinterested pupils
- Enables students to develop musical (particularly listening) and leadership skills
- Develops independent learning skills
- Enables students to demonstrate their musical potential
- Supports student progression in music
- Improves behaviour, focus and attendance, and has a positive impact on students' attitudes towards music in school
- Improves performance skills and develops student understanding of a range of musical genres
- Increases numbers of students electing to continue with music making outside the classroom
- Improves take up of GCSE/Key Stage 4 music
- Improves student attainment at Key Stage 3
- Has long-term and sustainable impact on teachers' practice, and often changes the way they deliver music learning in the classroom

The full report (*Survey of Musical Futures* (2008), Sue Hallam, Andrea Creech, Clare Sandford, Tiija Rinta, Katherine Shave) by the Institute of Education is available from **www.musicalfutures.org.uk/c/reports+ and+articles**. The findings of this report correlate with those of the Musical Futures pathfinders, and ongoing feedback from teachers and practitioners.

▶ HOW TO USE THIS PACK

This resource pack provides a starting point for Musical Futures, which should be personalised to suit the needs of your students, and your personal teaching style.

Newcomers to Musical Futures and to this resource pack should familiarise themselves with the background and philosophy of Musical Futures, before embarking on adapting the approaches in the classroom. The pamphlet *Personalising Music Learning* (David Price) was written at the culmination of the pathfinder projects, and places Musical Futures in the context of personalisation. If you are not already familiar with the background and philosophy of Musical Futures, this is a good place to start (download it from **www.musicalfutures.org.uk/c/pamphlets**).

INTRODUCTION

● FIRST EDITION

The first edition of the resource materials is an outcome of the work of the pathfinder projects.

It outlines the rationale, what happened, how the pathfinders developed the models, and the results. As the philosophy and approach of Musical Futures hasn't changed, many aspects of this second edition are similar to the first edition. However, the advice and guidance has been updated based on how we know teachers and practitioners develop Musical Futures in practice. Some of the material is therefore re-presented and updated here, alongside a range of new material developed by teachers and practitioners.

This edition focuses on what you should do and how you might consider doing it, rather than on 'what happened'. If you are interested in reading more about the pathfinder projects, the first edition is still available to download from **www.musicalfutures.org.uk/c/first+edition**.

● WEBSITE

A number of the projects refer to accompanying audio and video resource material, which is all stored on the Musical Futures website for download.

The website also has a function for teachers and practitioners to submit material, resources, and ideas surrounding Musical Futures (**www.musicalfutures.org.uk/c/teacher+created**). We would encourage you to submit any resources you develop for your own Musical Futures work to share and develop with other colleagues.

● PROJECT SNAPSHOTS

Throughout the materials we provide 'snapshots' for how you may consider structuring Musical Futures work over a number of lessons.

This assumes one 60-minute lesson per week, yet we know that in reality schools operate very different timetables. Therefore, these snapshots must only be treated as guides – we would expect teachers to be flexible in terms of student progress and how much time they have available for each project. Neither are these complete lesson plans – they simply give an indication of what might happen during a typical lesson.

▶ MUSICAL FUTURES OUTSIDE ENGLAND

Musical Futures was designed with the English curriculum and education system in mind. However, the pedagogical approaches of Musical Futures can be (and have been) adapted by schools, teachers and practitioners from across the UK and beyond.

We would like to encourage overseas colleagues to share their experiences of Musical Futures, and how it has been used in different contexts at (**www.musicalfutures.org.uk/c/teacher+created**). Throughout this pack we refer to the English education system, which is as follows:

Key Stage	Year	Age	Explanation
Foundation		3–5 years	
Key Stage 1	1 and 2	5–7 years	Music is a statutory part of the curriculum
Key Stage 2	3, 4, 5 and 6	7–11 years	Music is a statutory part of the curriculum
Key Stage 3	7	11–12 years	Music is a statutory part of the curriculum
	8	12–13 years	The majority of Musical Futures work takes place in Key Stage 3
	9	13–14 years	
Key Stage 4	10 and 11	14–16 years	Music becomes an optional subject, which is when GCSE music, or other qualifications, are opted for

Some schools start Key Stage 4 in Year 9, meaning that music is only statutory until the end of Year 8.

Following Key Stage 4, a number of schools have optional 6th forms where students can take A Levels, and a variety of other qualifications. At this point, many students opt to attend colleges of further education to pursue A Levels or vocational qualifications.

Implementing Musical Futures

You don't have to be approved by Musical Futures to use or adapt the approaches in your school or teaching situation. All of the principles and ideas can be developed by teachers and other music practitioners, often with little or no extra support or funding.

Here are some suggestions for how to get started with Musical Futures:

- Use the resource materials to decide the best starting point for your students (the first projects in the non-formal teaching and informal learning sections are generally good places to start)

- It is recommended that you initially trial Musical Futures with one or two classes/groups to see how they respond and to identify resource needs, before rolling out the approach further. Some schools begin by trialling Musical Futures as an out-of-hours activity, and then gradually bring the ideas into their mainstream curriculum

- Ensure that the school leadership team is familiar with the Musical Futures approach (see the section on advice for senior managers and Ofsted on page 203)

- Register online to receive updates about training, resources and events (**www.musicalfutures.org.uk/newsletter**)

Musical Futures is unlikely to work in the way it was intended if it is just used as a scheme of work, a quick fix for those difficult Year 9 lessons, or as a last resort. Each project, idea and approach to teaching and learning offers much scope for development, adaptation and personalisation, both to your needs and the needs of your students. However to ensure that the essence of Musical Futures isn't lost, referring back to the principles and ethos of what Musical Futures is trying to achieve is critical in justifying the reasons for taking it on.

In our Institute of Education survey (see **www.musicalfutures.org.uk/c/ reports+and+articles** for the full report), key expectations of those planning to implement Musical Futures were that it would:

- Increase motivation (52%)

- Provide a more stimulating curriculum (29%)

- Raise standards (22%)

- Enhance musical skills (17%)

- Provide professional development (16%)

- Increase the numbers of students taking GCSE Music (14%)

Musical Futures is unlikely to work in the way it was intended if it is just used as a scheme of work

▶ TAKING ON MUSICAL FUTURES

There is a misconception that teachers need to be fully skilled in and knowledgeable about rock, popular and urban styles of music to be able to run Musical Futures.

Teachers who have had success with Musical Futures have in many cases received a fairly formal training themselves, and this way of working is often completely new to them. Style and genre of music is not the focus with Musical Futures, rather the approach to teaching and learning.

Musical Futures teachers/practitioners should:

○ Be willing to help students pick up music by ear

○ Be willing to work across a broad range of styles, genres and instruments

○ Be willing to learn alongside students

○ Have a good relationship with students, and be able to create an environment of trust and respect

○ Be open to modelling, guiding and facilitating as part of their teaching style

○ Be able to respond to individual students' needs, even if this means lessons/projects have unexpected outcomes

The Institute of Education survey revealed that teachers who had implemented Musical Futures consistently reported that they:

○ Felt more confident about facilitating student learning in a range of musical genres, and teaching a range of instrumental skills

○ Found teaching music more enjoyable

○ Considered themselves more effective teachers

○ Engaged in more personalised teaching

○ Adopted a more practical approach in the classroom

Teachers who have had success with Musical Futures have in many cases received a fairly formal training themselves

▶ RESOURCES

Musical Futures can be implemented in most teaching situations, often with little or no extra funding.

Each project within this pack provides details of specific resources that are needed. These are only recommendations, and do not imply that a project cannot be attempted without the specified resources. However, in the long term, the following can help to effectively carry out Musical Futures:

○ Enough spaces for students to be able to work in small groups (not necessarily just practice rooms)

○ A variety of instruments (electronic and acoustic) to enable all students to have a hands-on music-making experience

IMPLEMENTING MUSICAL FUTURES

- Access to the expertise of other musicians and music leaders – for example older students within the school, peripatetic teachers, community musicians

- Some access to music technology for students to record and where appropriate remix and publish their work

Among teachers surveyed, the most commonly cited difficulties with implementing Musical Futures were space restrictions, and limited financial support for purchasing equipment. We have provided some advice and guidance for this in the Equipment and Music Technology (page 185) and Buildings and Space sections (page 194).

○ TIMETABLING

Many Musical Futures schools have explored the possibility of timetabling all music lessons for a year group in one day.

Benefits of this include:

- It is much more cost-effective to be able to offer 'whole-day' work to external musicians/practitioners

- Equipment/technology can be set up for a whole day, which can be more time effective

- After-school activities can be scheduled that directly link to the work that has taken place on that day, and that can also make use of any external musicians you have used

Increasingly, schools are experimenting with more flexible timetabling arrangements, such as scheduling music sessions in half-day blocks. This can enhance the experience for students, as wanting more time is frequently cited as something students feel would be beneficial. However, there has been equally successful practice observed within the more traditional one hour (or even 50 minutes) lesson format.

Increasingly, schools are experimenting with more flexible timetabling arrangements

▶ NATIONAL CURRICULUM

The National Curriculum has at its core that 'Music helps pupils understand themselves, relate to others and develop their cultural understanding, forging important links between home, school and the wider world', which correlates with the fundamental ethos of Musical Futures.

Musical Futures encourages the following, which are clearly stated in the National Curriculum:

- Students develop integrated performing, composing, improvising and listening skills
- Students participate, collaborate and work with others as musicians
- Students are able to build on their own interests and skills, take on different roles and responsibilities, and develop leadership skills
- Students critically engage with, review and analyse music, and are able to justify views and form opinions
- Students explore how to communicate through music
- Students perform in a range of contexts within and beyond the classroom
- Students develop understanding of a range of live and recorded music from different times and cultures
- Students make use of music technology
- Students understand the role of music and musicians in society, and work with a range of musicians
- Students work individually, in small groups and as a whole class
- Students make links between music and other areas of the curriculum

In addition to fulfilling the programmes of study for music, Musical Futures provides an abundance of opportunities for evidencing some of the wider aims of the new curriculum.

The personalised nature of much of Musical Futures means that it is possible to collect evidence of meeting the Every Child Matters outcomes, notably enjoying and achieving, staying safe and making a positive contribution. Personal Learning and Thinking Skills (PLTS) are at the centre of the drive to encourage independent learners in all aspects of school life. The aim is to encourage independent enquirers, creative thinkers, reflective learners, team workers, self managers and effective participants, all of which are embedded throughout Musical Futures. It is possible to go through every aspect of Musical Futures, including the principles of informal learning and the structures of all of the projects, to find examples of students working to develop these skills in their music lessons. Emphasis can then be placed on helping students to identify that they are working in this way through regular reflection and evaluation.

WEBLINK
The National Curriculum website (http://curriculum.qca.org.uk/key-stages-3-and-4/curriculum-in-action/index.aspx) has two case studies showing how Musical Futures meets the requirements of the National Curriculum ('Developing Musical Skills' and 'Personalised Learning Breathes Life Into Music').

IMPLEMENTING MUSICAL FUTURES

⊙ ASSESSMENT

Musical Futures provides ample opportunity for Assessment for Learning (AfL) strategies such as peer assessment, self assessment, formal and informal assessment, target setting, formative and summative assessment all within current Qualification and Curriculum Authority (www.qca.org.uk) assessment guidelines.

Equally important is tracking student progress and understanding. We give specific examples of how some of our Champion Schools have done this on (**www.musicalfutures.org.uk/c/teacher+created**). Similarly, some schools have also considered the issue of how to undertake baseline data collection in Year 7 in order to track students musically throughout Key Stage 3 (the Whole Class Instrumental Work: Year 7 section on page 76 gives an example of a programme that might enable you to collect this information), and to identify peer leaders at an early stage.

We recommend the use of audio and video recording throughout Musical Futures to capture students' work and to ensure that musical learning and progress can be effectively assessed. Using multiple assessment points (drawing on AfL strategies) within a lesson can be effective – for example, filming a performance, reviewing it with

NUMU

NUMU (**www.numu.org.uk**, see page 191) is an effective way of storing student's audio, video and reviews of their work.

IMPLEMENTING MUSICAL FUTURES

Audio and video material can be particularly powerful evidence to show your senior management team and/or Ofsted

the group, analysing areas for development, and then re-filming it for final grading, followed by ample opportunities for students to consolidate their learning. Audio and video material can then be demonstrated as exemplar work with future classes, and can be particularly powerful evidence to show your senior management team and/or Ofsted.

Ofsted's advice is that 'Good assessment requires a clear learning objective and a close focus on the progress of individuals in the class.... Recording the outcomes should enable work to be adapted so that all students have sufficient challenge and support.' (*From Making More of Music*, see **www.musicalfutures.org.uk/external+observers**). In this report Ofsted explains that the National Curriculum level descriptions are intended to describe a broad picture of attainment and understanding of the nature of music, with the first sentence of each level stating the musical understanding expected.

Because schools are developing Musical Futures in different ways and have their own school-based assessment policies, we have not published a separate set of assessment criteria. However, the following table shows **one** set of suggestions for ways in which you could illustrate to your students how they can progress through their Musical Futures learning.

We are starting to collect examples on **www.musicalfutures.org.uk/assessment** of assessment criteria that teachers have developed for Musical Futures.

IMPLEMENTING MUSICAL FUTURES

ASSESSMENT ILLUSTRATION

Level	Description	What you might see in Musical Futures lessons to reflect this PLEASE NOTE: THESE ARE JUST EXAMPLES – THE LEVELS NEED TO BE ASSESSED OVER A RANGE OF WORK	Musical Futures projects in which you might see this
Level 4	Students identify and explore the relationship between sounds and how music reflects different intentions.	Students learn to play a simple part on an instrument so they can play in a class band. Some pieces are learnt by ear (for example call and response), others from notations. Students are able to play their part in time with others, understand how their part relates to the overall intentions of the piece and the rest of the band, and are able to improvise phrases as part of the overall structure. They listen to a recording of their performance and are able to evaluate how well the performance has communicated the intentions of the piece, as well as being able to suggest improvements (for example via **www.numu.org.uk**).	See for example: Guide to Classroom Workshopping (page 47); Whole Class Instrumental Work: Year 7 (page 76); Image Junction (page 116).
Level 5	Students identify and explore musical devices and how music reflects time, place and culture.	Students learn to play a significant part on an instrument so they can play as part of a salsa band. They understand the significance of a clave beat in salsa, and are able to play in time with this. They are aware of how their own part relates to the rest of the band as well as to traditional musical devices and performing traditions found in Latin American culture. They are able to improvise solos as part of the overall structure of the piece. They listen to recordings of their performances and are able to compare them with recordings/video of other salsa pieces, identifying common features, and are able to refine their performances as a result, both purely musically and in terms of presentation skills appropriate for the music.	See for example: Whole Class Instrumental Work: Year 7 (page 76); Non-Western Music (page 95)
Level 6	Students identify and explore the different processes and contexts of selected musical styles, genres and traditions.	Students have a good understanding of the processes through which popular musicians learn, and understanding of the difference between this and other musical learning processes. They listen analytically to recordings of various musical styles/traditions, and are able to aurally identify the key elements of the musical texture, expression and structure. They are then able to recreate these key elements into their own performance using instruments and/or voices, with each student making subtle adjustments so that their part fits with and supports the overall group performance. They are able to use their understanding of the key elements of the musical style to improve their work and make it more stylistically appropriate. They compose their own music in different styles and genres, adopting key processes relevant to each style that they have identified through their analytical listening to recordings. Musical ideas are successfully sustained and developed.	See for example: In at the Deep End (page 144); Modelling Aural Learning (page 149); Informal Composing (page 154); Informal Learning with Other Musics (page 158).

Level	Description	What you might see in Musical Futures lessons to reflect this PLEASE NOTE: THESE ARE JUST EXAMPLES – THE LEVELS NEED TO BE ASSESSED OVER A RANGE OF WORK	Musical Futures projects in which you might see this
Level 7	Students discriminate between and explore musical conventions in, and influences on selected styles, genres and traditions.	Students are able to perform and compose pieces from different styles, genres and traditions and are clearly being guided by an aural memory of the music that they have listened to, showing an awareness of the different conventions (performing, compositional, contextual) and understanding of the musical influences for each style. They make a significant contribution to ensemble performances. They are able to do this both in styles set by the teacher and those they have chosen for themselves. For example students might: • Compose and perform a soul song with vocal inflections that clearly show aural memory and understanding of the music's roots in black musical culture AND • Listen to a Bollywood tune and use music technology to recreate it, using conventions of the style AND • Listen to the start of the Mozart clarinet concerto, identifying conventions such as appoggiaturas, phrasing, etc, then improvise a tune in the style of Mozart over the same chord sequence. Record this work and analyse others' work to see how close to the Mozartian style it is, then adapt, develop or extend the music to produce a version showing real understanding of the conventions used by Mozart	See for example: Guide to Songwriting (page 101); Informal Composing (page 154); Informal Learning with Other Musics (page 158).
Level 8	Students discriminate between and exploit the characteristics and expressive potential of selected musical resources, styles, genres and traditions.	In their overall work students have shown understanding of cultural context and the ability to exploit expressive **potential** across a **range** of different styles, traditions and genres. For example they may have: • Given exciting and convincing performances in a Taiko group of a piece they have structured themselves, with an excellent understanding of how to use Taiko conventions and principles such as Kata and Ki to make maximum impact • Composed and recorded a song about someone who feels that the world ignores them. The song apparently uses the traditional conventions of a ballad, but also challenges those conventions: as the song progresses music technology has been used to make the voice gradually fade out (and gain reverb) so that by the end it can be barely heard, and is overwhelmed by the instrumental backing	See for example: Non-Western Music (page 95); Guide to Songwriting (page 101); Informal Composing (page 154).
Exceptional performance	Students discriminate between and develop different interpretations.	Students can describe in detail how and why (for example) Jeff Buckley's *Hallelujah* is different to the X-Factor version, show understanding of the different musical traditions involved, and are able to perform different interpretations of the same song. Arising from this understanding, they produce their own convincing interpretation in a style that is consistent, personal to them and fully embraces the potential of other musicians involved and technology.	See for example: Band Instrumental Work (page 88); In at the Deep End (page 144); Modelling Aural Learning (page 149).

IMPLEMENTING MUSICAL FUTURES

◗ LEARNING OUTCOMES

Learning outcomes are not identified throughout these materials, as part of the informal nature of Musical Futures learning is the scope it holds for unexpected, unplanned musical and personal outcomes.

The advice Ofsted provides in the *Making More of Music* report, is that it is important for students to understand what the focus of the learning is, why they are learning in a Musical Futures style, and for the teacher to be clear about what the broad objectives are that students should aim to achieve throughout each project.

◗ MEETING ALL STUDENTS' NEEDS

Musical Futures has been effective with all young people, no matter what their background and prior musical experience.

Musical Futures is designed to be personalised by teachers to meet the changing needs of individual students as they work through projects, whether they are learning, behavioural or physical difficulties, or if they are particularly gifted and talented in music. The following is an indication of who might be the Gifted and Talented, and Special Educational Needs students in a music classroom, and suggests how to guide these students through Musical Futures so that they can progress at their own level.

GIFTED AND TALENTED

Gifted and Talented students in music may be those who:

- Have excellent natural ears and can easily pick out layers of music and play back
- Are able to play more than one instrument
- Are self-taught musicians and/or composers/songwriters
- Have access to music at home via a parent, friend or relative
- Have had instrumental lessons in a traditional one-to-one or small group format and are notation literate

Strategies for challenging these students (although students may find these themselves!):

- Encourage them to take responsibility for supporting less able or less experienced members of the group/class
- For those who usually play only by notation, encourage them to work aurally; and for those who usually work aurally, encourage them to work by notation
- Work on instruments with which they are unfamiliar
- Learn to play melodies, riffs or pieces in different keys
- Extend learning with an instrumental teacher, extra-curricular project or at home

Musical Futures is designed to be personalised by teachers to meet the changing needs of individual students

IMPLEMENTING MUSICAL FUTURES

- Search online for help and further resources
- Undertake an individual project in addition to the work the rest of the class are following

SPECIAL EDUCATIONAL NEEDS

Literacy and numeracy issues don't necessarily impact on progress in Musical Futures as long as students are given regular opportunities for verbal feedback.

There are, of course, a great variety of complex special educational needs, but some general strategies for working with students are:

- Students may need help finding the right group and integrating, if they have problems working with others
- Dyspraxic students may need support with holding instruments or with initial instrument choice
- Students may struggle to hear layers in the music and need help to get started (either finding the first note or learning a simple riff)
- Students may find it difficult to remember things from one lesson to the next and need a diary (aural or written) to record progress
- Students may need support to sustain concentration through regular visits by the teacher, tasks broken down, or 'time out'
- Students with emotional or behavioural difficulties may need additional supervision, for example by a teaching assistant

A guide to working with students in EBD and MLD schools, produced by pathfinder schools in Hertfordshire is available from **www. musicalfutures.org.uk/c/reports+and+articles**.

◐ BRINGING MUSICIANS INTO THE CLASSROOM

Musical Futures sets out to break down some of the traditional barriers between classroom, instrumental teaching, the extended curriculum and students' own interests, and encourages partnerships between schools and external providers wherever possible.

Musical Futures offers opportunities to bring a range of music expertise in a variety of contexts into the classroom, whether through musicians supporting classroom teachers, or by leading sessions (curricular and extra-curricular) themselves.

Music practitioners are increasingly required to be flexible to working in different ways with young people. Therefore if a school is interested in bringing musicians into the classroom there are a number of agencies who can help. MusicLeader (**www.musicleader.net**), Soundsense (**www.soundsense.org**), and increasingly some Music Services offer training and development for music practitioners to be able to work

SECTION 1: INTRODUCTION

in a variety of settings. MusicLeader and Soundsense (with support from Musical Futures) has developed a 'Code of Practice' for music practitioners – a framework setting out six key professional principles to adhere to in order to deliver safe, responsible and quality work.

Many universities and initial teacher training institutions make their PGCE students aware of Musical Futures. PGCE students are therefore likely to be coming to school placements with ideas about Musical Futures, and are in an ideal position to help and support teachers in the classroom.

CODE OF PRACTICE
The Code of Practice, along with details of related training, is available from **www.musicleader.net**.

○ STUDENTS AS LEADERS

A particularly strong characteristic of Musical Futures is the way that some students emerge as peer leaders.

This tends to happen intrinsically as part of Musical Futures lessons, with more able students willingly helping their peers. This type of peer coaching often has a greater impact than advice offered from a teacher. Students who naturally emerge as peer leaders through Musical Futures may not always be the ones teachers would expect (for example they may not be on the Gifted and Talented register).

Teachers and practitioners have drawn on this and support it in various ways. For example:

- ○ By encouraging gifted and talented students to spend a lesson/lessons working with other students in the class to develop skills on specific instruments. This can help students to realise that learning to lead is as important a skill to be developed as musical skills

- ○ Inviting older students from within the school to demonstrate/run a workshop for younger students, and to help them with their work

- ○ By assigning specific students a leadership responsibility in their group/class, for example band manager, band coach, sound engineer, etc

We would strongly encourage teachers to support, acknowledge and encourage peer leaders. Assessment should take into account any leadership roles the students have taken on, and qualifications such as the BTEC and Arts Award (**www.artsaward.org.uk**) can provide accreditation for students leading others. Musical Futures links particularly well with Arts Award – a national qualification which supports young people to develop as artists and arts leaders. A document outlining the potential links between Musical Futures and Arts Award is available on **www.musicalfutures.org.uk/mf+and+arts+award**.

Students who naturally emerge as peer leaders through Musical Futures may not always be the ones teachers would expect

◗ TECHNOLOGY

FURTHER READING

Electrifying Music is a case study of integrating ICT into music education (available from **www.musicalfutures. org.uk/electrifying+music**) and the *Creative Guide to Music Technology* takes teachers unsure of music technology through some basic processes (available from **www.musicalfutures.org.uk/ equipment+technology**).

ICT and music technology are integral to Musical Futures work, and can be used throughout.

Recording, uploading, mixing, sequencing, sampling, creating CDs/ MP3s, using electronic equipment and web-based technology is part of what many students do in their own time. It is therefore important that this is reflected in Musical Futures classroom practice. The Equipment and Music Technology section (page 185) provides some basic advice and guidance for integrating technology into Musical Futures, including using NUMU (**www.numu.org.uk**). However, as music technology continues to change and develop so rapidly, few references are made to specific hardware, software or technologies so that schools can adapt resources accordingly.

◗ BUILDING ON PRIOR MUSICAL EXPERIENCE

One of the most significant developments in primary music education in the last decade has been the success of the Key Stage 2 Whole Class Instrumental and Vocal Tuition programme, popularly known as Wider Opportunities.

The cornerstone of this programme is that every child in Key Stage 2 gets the chance to learn a musical instrument, free of charge and in normal lesson time. Initially piloted in 12 local authorities in 2002–03, the Department for Children, Schools and Families (DCSF) has now set targets for all schools with Key Stage 2 children to have a Wider Opportunities programme by 2011. Furthermore, the national singing strategy 'Sing Up' (**www.singup.org.uk**) encourages singing programmes in all primary schools.

The DCSF has charged secondary schools with 'giving urgent attention to the impact of the KS2 programme on pupils who transfer to secondary school – developing new models where necessary'.

FURTHER READING

See DCSF (2008) *Music Education and the Music Grant Aspirations, Support and Delivery.*

Therefore, secondary music teachers will inevitably start to encounter the challenge of how to build upon the strengths and past work of the Wider Opportunities and Sing Up programmes, to ensure more consistent provision in the transition between Key Stages 2 and 3. As all Wider Opportunities programmes are different, it is important to establish what is happening in feeder primaries. Building information about the Wider Opportunities initiatives in your main feeder schools, together with the opportunity to see music in action in a primary school is invaluable in ensuring that music provision does not simply 'start again' in Year 7.

You may expect to see the following generic skills, knowledge and experience from students who have experienced a Wider Opportunities programme at Key Stage 2:

IMPLEMENTING MUSICAL FUTURES

- Ability to listen to and copy rhythms using instruments and voices, play pieces by ear, and play along to a live and/or recorded musical backing
- Ability to play instruments with different techniques, a range of dynamics, basic playing techniques (for example tonguing/bowing etc) and a range of notes (for example from open strings to 1st/2nd finger on violin, or 5–6 notes on trumpet/flute/clarinet, etc)
- Sing in unison and two (or more) parts
- Knowledge of music in a range of styles, from different cultures, times and places
- Ability to improvise and compose simple melodic material, using a range of pitch, dynamics and techniques
- Ability to structure simple musical ideas to create whole pieces
- Ability to follow simple notation (such as piece structure, or note names, sometimes with rest signs, dynamics, words to remember rhythms, etc)
- Experience of performing as an ensemble (sometimes in public), often with more than one musical part, and of following a conductor (especially for entries, coming off together, dynamics, structure)

Musical Futures naturally complements these programmes, and there are many synergies between them. Our Whole Class Instrumental Work: Year 7 project on page 76 provides some practical ideas for a Wider Opportunities/Musical Futures 'hybrid' programme. In addition, the Paul Hamlyn Foundation will be working with other partners in the music education sector to launch a new national initiative to improve young people's experience of Key Stage 2–Key Stage 3 transition in music and to identify and spread effective practice in this area. Further information about this will be available from **www.phf.org.uk** and the Musical Futures website.

○ MUSICAL FUTURES AND OTHER INITIATIVES

Musical Futures was intended to integrate with existing classroom practice as well as other major initiatives in music education.

It was designed with the English National Curriculum in mind, and sits alongside the Secondary Strategy Key Stage 3 Music Programme. It has contributed to the development of, and continues to support the work of, the Music Manifesto. Musical Futures has an area on the Teaching Music website (**www.teachingmusic.org.uk/musicalfutures**) and encourages Champion Schools and other teachers to debate and share Musical Futures resources in this online teaching and learning community.

FURTHER READING
Musical Futures and the Secondary National Strategy Key Stage 3 Programme (available from **www.musicalfutures. org.uk/c/reports+and+articles**) provides a comparative analysis of the two initiatives.

▶ KEY STAGE 4 AND BEYOND

Musical Futures teachers typically witness a rise in the numbers of students wanting to continue with music making at Key Stage 4.

This often results in teachers modifying their approaches to teaching and learning in Key Stage 4 and beyond, to draw on some of the non-formal and informal teaching and learning practices of Musical Futures. Furthermore, the profile of students entering Key Stage 4 can differ from pre-Musical Futures, and this has in many cases led teachers to re-consider their Key Stage 4 provision. Teachers have responded to this through the following:

- Re-assessing the qualifications on offer at Key Stage 4, for example, alongside GCSE many teachers now offer more vocational courses such as BTEC, as well as courses such as Arts Award and Rockschool Access to Music

- Putting 'fast-track' measures in place towards the end of Key Stage 3 to allow for personalised routes through GCSE music qualifications

- Adjusting teaching and learning styles at Key Stage 4, so that more informal and non-formal learning/teaching occurs, ensuring a smoother transition for students

- Taking the ideas behind Musical Futures projects and adapting them to suit the KS4 syllabuses (for example informal learning around minimalism, etc)

Co-constructing a Curriculum

All Musical Futures projects are designed with student voice and pupil choice at the centre. Throughout Musical Futures there are opportunities for the views, opinions, interests and preferred learning styles of students to play a vital part in determining how sessions progress – giving scope for teachers/practitioners to react by personalising projects as a result. Student voice is the fundamental reason why there is no one 'typical' Musical Futures project in any school – good teachers adapt and personalise the models as appropriate.

In the informal learning model (see page 130), we advocate that teachers seek their students' views and opinions of the informal learning pedagogies as they go along. This will help teachers develop their understanding of students' learning experiences, motivations, and their own perceptions of how their skills and knowledge are developing. Where appropriate, students' views can also guide teachers in adjusting their approaches (for example by adding skills-building sessions, performance opportunities, additional musician support in the classroom, etc). However, the informal learning model focuses on the teaching-and-learning strategies themselves – i.e. on *pedagogy*. This is distinct from the focus of our original pathfinder projects led by Nottingham (the Whole Curriculum Approach) and Leeds (Personalising Extra Curricular Learning) both of which involved students in the co-construction of the *curriculum* and extended activities.

The following information on co-construction is based particularly on the approach the Nottingham Musical Futures team took to design a curriculum with students from scratch, and it covers some of the potential benefits and starting points for how you could approach co-construction in your school. Some of the projects developed as a result of the Nottingham 'Whole Curriculum Approach' are outlined in this pack, for example those that incorporate being in a band, playing in different styles/genres, and playing a variety of different instruments (see Image Junction page 116; Band Instrumental Work page 88 and Non-Western Music page 95).

Key outcomes of co-construction should be to identify and establish effective and sustainable pathways, opportunities and methods of accreditation through Musical Futures work. These should fit with the skills, interests and aspirations of students and connect with the many, not the few, in order to raise student motivation, achievement and self esteem.

WHOLE CURRICULUM APPROACH
The first edition of the teacher pack (see **www.musicalfutures.org.uk/c/first+edition**) provides an illustration of the full curriculum developed by the Nottingham Musical Futures team as a direct result of student consultation. The framework for the Leeds consultation process is provided in Developing Extra-curricular Provision on page 174.

⊙ BENEFITS

Potential benefits of co-constructing a curriculum with your students are that it:

- Enables students to take ownership over their music learning, as the curriculum becomes influenced by the result of asking students what they want from their music lessons
- Makes tangible connections with students' musical lives outside school and moves students' musical experiences beyond the classroom
- Achieves a balance between what students already know they want to do and new experiences
- Makes active music making something that all students are involved in
- Gives opportunities to make sustained progress in key areas, to develop new musical skills and reinforce existing skills

⊙ PROCESS

Incorporating co-construction into your music department can range from personalising lessons based on the needs of individual students/classes, to enabling content and repertoire to be determined by your students, to restructuring and re-building your curriculum every year, keeping it revitalised in response to feedback from student evaluations.

The Nottingham Musical Futures pathfinder explored the following with students:

- Finding ways of involving students in real musical activity, in genuine musical situations and environments
- Discovering and then supporting students' interests and preferred modes of learning outside school
- Drawing on the expertise of musicians in order to give students exposure to a range of experiences
- Integrating good practice from classroom teaching, instrumental teaching, extra-curricular music and community music

CO-CONSTRUCTING A CURRICULUM

EXAMPLE OF A PROCESS FOR CO-CONSTRUCTING A CURRICULUM:

| Provide taster sessions | Consult with students based on their experiences | Design a curriculum | Refine with students | Implement |

A key consideration when designing a curriculum is how extra-curricular learning can be built in to enable follow-on activities that are directly relevant to all students. Developing Extra-curricular Provision (page 174) provides some ideas for how to construct a programme of extra-curricular activities based on a system of diagnosing, planning and reviewing students' needs.

◆ CONSULTING WITH STUDENTS

Consultation can be most effective when students have something to base their experiences on.

Students will undoubtedly have ideas about what they would like to do, but these are likely to be limited to (or reacting against) their prior experiences, which may be narrow in range, or based on unrealistic expectations influenced by the media.

Therefore, to build a meaningful curriculum with student input, consider initially providing students with a range of practical musical experiences that:

- ◆ Provide access to a range of instruments and technology
- ◆ Demonstrate different learning styles
- ◆ Involve a combination of large group, small group and individual work
- ◆ Expose students to musicians outside of the classroom

Interview samples of students in small groups, assessing what they liked, didn't like, what they learnt, how they preferred to learn, how

CO-CONSTRUCTING A CURRICULUM

they would like to progress and so on. It is also useful to explore musical experiences that they would like to have in music lessons and/ or out-of-school. Useful responses might come from completing the phrase 'It would be great if...'

During the pilot phase of Musical Futures, and in schools since, responses from students tend to be generic, rather than specific about styles and genres. For example:

- To experience all sorts of varieties of music
- To use music technology
- To use a recording studio
- To play with other people
- To learn to play something
- Stay to try instruments after school
- To have access to rehearsal space
- To perform/have a concert
- To take part in competitions
- To go into more depth about some types of music rather than changing every couple of weeks
- To have a mix of 'organised' and 'what you want'

However, responses will of course vary due to the personalised nature of Musical Futures projects.

Co-construction and consultation should be an ongoing process – it is not necessarily simply a case of asking students what they want and then throwing all of your ideas out of the window.

Building on feedback from consultation with students it should be possible to mix and match Musical Futures projects to meet student needs as appropriate. There is also plenty of scope for creating new projects to truly personalise any curriculum.

Embedding Musical Futures

Musical Futures in reality looks different in every school. Some teachers implement Musical Futures throughout the course of an entire academic year. However, many teachers alternate Musical Futures work with other provision, or apply the Musical Futures ethos to their overall approach to teaching and learning.

We do not advocate one particular way of following Musical Futures, as it depends entirely on individual schools, teachers and most importantly students. However, the following three tables are illustrations of ways in which Musical Futures can integrate into a Key Stage 3 curriculum:

1. An example of how Musical Futures could be implemented across the whole of Key Stage 3

2. A Key Stage 3 plan from Monks Walk School, Hertfordshire

3. A Key Stage 3 plan from Fred Longworth School, Wigan

Please note: where units of work relate directly to a Musical Futures project within this pack we have provided cross references to illustrate this.

EXAMPLE 1: MUSICAL FUTURES ACROSS KEY STAGE 3

YEAR 7

Half Term 1

Whole Class Instrumental Work: Year 7 (see page 76)

HT2–5

A programme of activities, such as that outlined in the Whole Class Instrumental Work: Year 7 section (see page 76) that involves students in whole class, practical music making, and introduces them to skills and knowledge needed in Years 8/9. Incorporate consultation with students throughout Year 7 that helps to shape Year 8/9 programmes

HT6

Guide to Classroom Workshopping (see page 47)

YEAR 8

Half Term 1

Guide to Classroom Workshopping (see page 47)

HT2

Non-Western Music (see page 95)

HT3

Band Instrumental Work (see page 88)

HT4

Music technology: sequencing, sampling, looping

HT5

Image Junction (see page 116)

HT6

Band Instrumental Work (see page 88). Culminating in public performance

YEAR 9

Half Term 1

In at the Deep End (see page 144)

HT2

Modelling Aural Learning (see page 149)

HT3

Skills building work. Revisit In at the Deep End

HT4

Informal Composing (see page 154)/Songwriting (see page 101)

HT5

Informal Learning with Other Musics (see page 158)

HT6

Students prepare for and perform in Year 9 'Battle of the Bands' concert, using work they have done during the year

EMBEDDING MUSICAL FUTURES

EXAMPLE 2: MONKS WALK SCHOOL, HERTFORDSHIRE

"At Monks Walk, we see Musical Futures as two separate initiatives. The first is a selection of projects which pupils work through where musical learning is integrated through performing, listening, composing and evaluating, and includes the informal learning units for Year 9. The second is more of an ethos within the department where teachers diagnose, model and facilitate, learners engage aurally as well as visually and work in friendship groups throughout. We place an emphasis on student voice, sharing of exemplary work and the development of personalised routes through music learning from Key Stages 3–5." (Anna Gower, Head of Music)

Monks Walk School is a Musical Futures Champion School

YEAR 7

Half Term 1	HT2	HT3	HT4	HT5	HT6
Elements of Music and Baseline Tests Students learn the *Song for Peace* in small groups by listening to and copying CDs. Teacher assesses students and retains information for tracking purposes. Whole year group performs in assembly	**Graphic Scores** Using *Stripsody* as a stimulus students compose a haunted house piece for Halloween and notate graphically	**House Music Song** Students choose and learn a song and perform in the house music competition as a form group	**Gamelan** Students are introduced to music from different cultures, and learn to compose and perform using a pentatonic scale and repeated patterns	**Stomp!** Students put together group Stomp! performances (junk percussion)	**Rhythms of the World** Carousel of introductory activities: samba band, taiko drumming, African drumming/singing as a whole class, and performance at the end of the project
MF Links 1) Prepares students for small group work 2) Introduces students to listening to and copying CDs 3) Introduces students to performing as a whole class as well as in small groups	**MF Links** 1) Composing collaboratively in groups 2) Learning about graphic notation as a means of recording musical ideas (links particularly to Image Junction, see page 116)	**MF Links** 1) Develops performing skills and increases vocal confidence 2) Links to In at the Deep End (see page 144)	**MF Links** Links to Non-Western Musics (see page 95), and Informal Learning with Other Musics (see page 158)	**MF Links** 1) Students learn rhythmic notation, develop performance skills and rhythmic composition 2) Students develop awareness of venue and audience – links with Non-Western Music (see page 95)	**MF Links** 1) Students increase confidence in performing in a range of different musical styles 2) Links to Non-Western Music (see page 95) 3) Learning non-western music via aural/oral learning leading to a performance

EMBEDDING MUSICAL FUTURES

YEAR 8

Half Term 1	HT2	HT3	HT4	HT5	HT6
Blues Students perform 12-bar blues bass and chords, and jazz improvisation using blues scales	**Pachelbel/Pop go the Classics** Students perform Pachelbel's Canon with multiple layers/different styles. They write a rap using Pachelbel as a backing sample	**Musicals** Students learn and perform an excerpt from a musical. Links to house music competition, and students upload their work onto NUMU. Integrates dance, drama and music.	**Fusions: Indian Raga/ Bhangra** Students listen to and perform a range of music which combines two or more cultures (for example bhangra), building in Western influences (dance rhythms, samples etc)	**Band Carousel** Students learn keyboards, bass, guitar and drums on a band carousel model	**Film Music** Students learn about leitmotif and underscore, choose a DVD and scene, and set to music in small groups using laptops
MF Links Students learn chords, bass lines and improvisation skills – needed for the informal learning approach in Year 9	**MF Links** 1) Links with Guide to Songwriting (see page 101) 2) Learning how to make a piece of classical music 'their own' links to Informal Learning with Other Musics (see page 158)	**MF Links** 1) Developing singing and performance skills 2) Use of NUMU 3) Student choice of song links to In at the Deep End (see page 144)	**MF Links** 1) Developing singing and performance skills 2) Links with Informal Learning with Other Musics (see page 158) and Non-Western Music (see page 95)	**MF Links** Band Instrumental Work (see page 88)	**MF Links** Image Junction (see page 116)

YEAR 9

Half Term 1	HT2	HT3	HT4	HT5	HT6
In at the Deep End (see page 144)	**Modelling Aural Learning** (see page 149)	**Informal Composing** (see page 154)	**Copyright and the Music Industry** Using Soundrights web resource (www. soundrights.co.uk) students research the music industry and find out how to copyright their own song	**Image Junction** (see page 116)	**Informal Learning with Other Musics** (see page 158)

EMBEDDING MUSICAL FUTURES

EXAMPLE 3: FRED LONGWORTH HIGH SCHOOL, WIGAN

"In our curriculum at Fred Longworth High School we try to incorporate the main concepts of Musical Futures alongside a whole-school initiative to introduce theme-based schemes of work that are skills based (a particular focus in Year 7). The influence of Musical Futures and particularly the concept of personalised learning permeates all of our schemes of work. We have moved towards a way of teaching and learning that gives students the skills and materials they need, but that allows them the freedom to be creative without setting too many boundaries. It is also important to give them choice – whether this is in their role within a group or the instrument they play." (Martin Ainscough, Head of Music)

Fred Longworth High School is a Musical Futures Champion School

YEAR 7

Half Term 1	HT2	HT3	HT4	HT5	HT6
Bridging Unit	**Respect and Elements of Music**	**JunKit**	**Understanding Notation**	**British Culture**	**Other Cultures**
Baseline assessment for new Year 7 Students. The unit looks at where students are currently, and assesses vocal performance; composition; listening skills	Students are shown a picture of a house and asked to compose music that fits this picture. Further information is released about the house and people that live there – how will this information change their compositions? Performances are recorded and played at the Christmas concert	Rhythmic performance unit using 'trash' instruments. Students perform a 'Stomp!' style whole class routine, then working in small groups they compose their own ostinatos leading to small group performances and peer appraisal. Students are encouraged to incorporate drama and dance into Stomp! routines	Individual performance based unit, focusing on traditional staff and graphic notation and keyboard work. Students learn to read treble clef notation, and perform simple pieces on keyboard	Students take pictures of the local town and create a collage of pictures using 'MovieMaker' or 'iMovie' to which they will add appropriate samples in sequencer package, may interview local elderly people and include in collage. Videos uploaded to NUMU	Students learn a piece of Bhangra (from appropriate notation) focusing on developing ensemble performance skills – including singing
MF Links	**MF Links**	**MF Links**	**MF Links**	**MF Links**	**MF Links**
Introduces students to integrating performing, composing and listening skills	Develops composing and performing skills	1) Students learn rhythmic notation, develop performance skills and rhythmic composition 2) Students develop awareness of venue and audience – links with Non-Western Music (see page 95)	Students learn how to use various notations, understanding how to write music down for MF work	1) Setting samples to a film links to Image Junction (see page 116) 2) Students build music based around something relevant to them 3) Use of NUMU	1) Developing singing and performance skills 2) Links with Non-Western Music (see page 95) and Informal Learning with Other Musics (see page 158)

YEAR 8

Half Term 1	HT2	HT3	HT4	HT5	HT6
Band skills 1	**Rhythms of the World**	**Structure**	**Image Junction**	**Songwriting**	**Blues**
Students are 'talent spotted' into bands, playing guitar, bass, keyboard, vocals, and drums. Performance recorded and uploaded to NUMU	Samba and Taiko – develop ensemble rhythmic performance skills. Students experience playing both genres of music as a whole class and in small groups. They compare both genres looking at cultural context. Students make masks to wear during Samba performances.	Unit looking at various structures within music. Focusing on variation theme, students listen to various examples, and then compose their own modern variation of a chosen piece	Students will look at the relationship of music and film. Using Logic to compose their own music to a short horror clip. Students learn informally – deciding what composers do to enhance a visual picture, then trying to apply these principles to their own movie clip	Composition-based activity focusing on lyrics and chord progressions. Look at various styles of music, focusing on protest songs – use current issues in the news to develop their own protest song lyrics (local or national). Students will learn about chords and create their own chord structure. Final performance of the song is recorded and uploaded to NUMU. ICT is used to help pupils hear chord progression (for example Jamstation)	Introduction to vocal traditions of the blues, and the slave trade. Students look at the development of the 12-bar blues and improvisation through both individual and small group performance. Students develop vocal skills, guitars and keyboards are also used
MF Links	**MF Links**	**MF Links**	**MF Links**	**MF Links**	**MF Links**
1) Band Instrumental Work (see page 88) 2) Use of NUMU	1) Students increase confidence in performing in a range of different musical styles 2) Links to Non-Western Music (see page 95)	Learning how to make a piece of classical music 'their own' links to Informal Learning with Other Musics (see page 158)	1) Informal learning model (see page 130) 2) Image Junction (see page 116)	1) Songwriting (see page 101) 2) Use of NUMU	Students learn chords, bass lines and improvisation skills needed for the informal learning approach

EMBEDDING MUSICAL FUTURES

EXAMPLE 3: FRED LONGWORTH HIGH SCHOOL, WIGAN (CONTINUED)

YEAR 9

Half Term 1	HT2	HT3	HT4	HT5	HT6
Music for Adverts By watching/listening to current adverts students try to unpick how composers write music that encourages the target audience to buy a product or service. Using ICT students compose their own music for their chosen advert and add a voice-over	**Solo Performance** Students choose an instrument and work to create their own solo performance. Range of pieces provided, or students can select their own piece. Final recording uploaded to NUMU	**Band Skills 2** Students again work in small bands using bass, guitar, drums, keyboard and vocals. Given a choice of 4/5 songs with a CD students choose a track and create their own version within their band from listening and copying their track from a CD. Culminates in a 'Battle of the Bands' style performance – other classes watch/vote. Upload to NUMU	**Instrumental Skills** ICT-based unit using Gigajam software. Students work independently through units, setting their own learning pace. The scheme of work culminates in small group performances of the tracks they have learnt through the software. Students are assessed using the assessment scheme built into the software	**Hip-Hop 1** The unit begins by looking at *Stan* by Eminem and Dido. Students comment on each musician and make comparisons between the two. Using keyboards Students learn and perform the *Stan* song	**Hip-Hop 2** ICT-based unit on Hip-Hop. Students use Garage Band or Logic software to create their own Hip-Hop composition. Throughout the unit students learn about structure within this genre of music, and gain ICT skills in using and manipulating samples
MF Links Bringing together students' experiences of music out of school (through media) and in school	**MF Links** 1) Student voice and choice 2) Informal learning model (see page 130) 3) Developing performing skills 4) Use of NUMU	**MF Links** 1) Band Instrumental Work (see page 88) 2) Modelling Aural Learning (see page 149) 3) Use of NUMU 4) Integrating performing, composing, listening	**MF Links** Informal, personalised approach to learning	**MF Links** 1) Modelling Aural Learning (see page 149) 2) Working with music that is familiar and relevant to students	**MF Links** 1) Modelling Aural Learning (see page 149) 2) Working with music that is familiar and relevant to students

Non-formal Teaching and Musical Futures

Introduction

In the early piloting of Musical Futures the development team were regularly asked to give a simple, one-sentence definition – a summation of how the approaches were different. That was a challenging task, as our pioneering pathfinder teams were trialling a complex series of actions, which spanned a wide spectrum of teacher/practitioner approaches.

Perhaps the most radical of those actions, and the ones that advocated little or no instruction from the teacher in the first few lessons, were those that became known as 'informal learning' (see page 130 for the informal learning model developed by Professor Lucy Green). These approaches were soon taken up by a large number of schools.

Yet Musical Futures has always recommended a *range* of teaching and learning strategies, according to the needs and interests of students, with the constant desired outcome of the teacher/practitioner to make music learning as practical an activity as possible, done 'with' and 'by' students, not 'to' and 'for' them.

ROLE OF THE TEACHER/PRACTITIONER

Through the original pathfinder projects we were able to bring together a range of practitioners (teachers, community musicians, instrumental tutors and peer leaders) to gain a better understanding of their pedagogical approaches. They worked in a variety of learning settings: skills-based workshops; group instrumental classes; exploratory composition/song writing sessions and group improvisation. Through working with each other, we saw shifts in their approaches that we have collectively categorised as 'non-formal teaching'. It's a term that has obvious limitations (not least in conjuring images of 'casual-ness') but it signals a shift in philosophy, as well as a desire to find a unifying *practice* common to a variety of music leaders (and their expertise), rather than the *context* (formal, non-formal and informal).

Non-formal teaching (as we illustrate in this section) has a number of common characteristics:

- An inclusive approach to music making, lowering entry barriers (for example, by not making notation a hurdle to be overcome before a student can play)

- A belief in group-based activities in performing, listening, composing and improvising

- A sense of immediacy and exploration

- An opportunity for tacit learning – music being 'caught' not 'taught' – music leaders may play a lot, and explain very little

- A more democratic view of learning – utilising the skills within the group through peer learning, teachers shedding the mantle of 'expert', students and teachers co-constructing content and objectives for sessions

- Opportunities to develop non-cognitive skills, such as responsibility, empathy, support for others, creativity and improvising to find solutions

A DISCIPLINE IN ITSELF

In trying to bring into the classroom some of the passion and excitement that exists in young people's lives outside the classroom, much of Musical Futures has drawn inspiration from some of the principles and best practices of community music.

Community music leaders, over the past 25 years, have been developing and refining a set of techniques and approaches that are highly effective in revealing young people's innate creativity and musicality. When led by a skilled practitioner, a typical music workshop is often a highly social, spontaneous and creative experience. In the hands of many secondary music teachers such qualities are also present. Conventionally trained musicians often attribute the success of group workshops to the personal qualities of the music leader: terms like 'charisma' become over-used descriptors. In fact, there are transferable skills and techniques outlined here, which *anyone* can develop.

The Guildhall School of Music and Drama has been at the forefront of documenting these ways of working for some time. In the first edition of the teacher resource materials we set Sean Gregory (Director of Guildhall's CONNECT programme) a challenge: show us how simple group-developed games and exercises can, in large groups, be collectively shaped into satisfying musical performances. While people were inspired by the end results of this approach to non-formal teaching, they felt that simpler starting points were needed. Therefore in this edition, Tim Steiner has created some classroom resources to support teachers looking to start working with group-based improvisation and composition (see page 47).

David Stoll has provided some simple but effective advice for teachers supporting students' songwriting (see page 101). In addition to revising some of the classroom projects pioneered in the first edition by the Leeds and Nottingham pathfinders, Ian Burton (Head of Nottingham City Music Service) has shared their successful whole-class instrumental teaching model for Year 7, which supports the transition from Wider Opportunities to Musical Futures (see page 76).

GETTING STARTED

In this section there are some examples of what we mean by non-formal teaching. Most of them rely upon teachers and practitioners facilitating large-group music-making experiences, enabling students to access real instruments in real-world contexts and integrating listening, improvising, composing and performing. Collectively, these resources provide a framework rather than a rigid set of instructions.

FURTHER READING

There are various guides to non-formal music leading, for example the *Community Music Handbook* edited by Peter Moser and George McKay, and *Living Music* by Rod Paton (www.lifemusic.org). If you feel you would benefit from face-to-face training in this area, there are many courses available through the national training development network MusicLeader (www.musicleader.net) and also from the Guildhall School of Music and Drama (www.gsmd.ac.uk/music/introduction/continuing_professional_development.html)

For more information on the outcomes of the Guildhall CONNECT work see *Transforming Musical Leadership* (pamphlet and film) and *Simply CONNECT* available to download from www.musicalfutures.org.uk/c/pamphlets.

INTRODUCTION

We strongly encourage you to see everything in this section as a **starting point only**. You should bring your own particular strengths, as a musician and educator, to personalising them for the needs of your students. When you feel confident working 'non-formally', devise your own projects and techniques that explore your own creativity, as well as that of your students.

We would recommend that you begin with the Guide to Classroom Workshopping project (page 47), especially if you are new to working non-formally, as it may well affect your interpretation of the other projects in this section.

Guide to Classroom Workshopping

This section is designed to introduce teachers/
practitioners to the process of large-group composition.
By creating a clear framework for the first few lessons,
we hope that you will gain the confidence to attempt
this approach, integrating and embedding it into your
classroom practice.

The techniques highlighted here are those developed
at the Guildhall School of Music and Drama
(**www.gsmd.ac.uk/connect**). Over the past two
decades they have established solid pedagogical
foundations for this type of work, exemplified by their
CONNECT Ensembles. The original film, commissioned
by Musical Futures, demonstrates Guildhall CONNECT's
practices, illustrating the process from warm-up exercises
through to final performance. If you are completely new to
the concept of creative workshop techniques, we strongly
advise that you view the film (at **www.musicalfutures.org.
uk/classroom+workshopping**) before embarking on this
section.

USING THE MATERIAL

The two mini projects that follow explore the initial stages of facilitating
group composition. The process is detailed in step-by-step fashion,
supported by accompanying film clips.

These materials illustrate a process that should work for practitioners
relatively inexperienced at leading creative ensembles. Each project begins
with non-instrumental warm-ups that prepare students for listening,
improvising, composing, arranging and performing activities. The projects
demonstrate how small musical ideas can be developed into complete
compositions.

While the instructions illustrate the direction a creative process could
take, they are not designed to be followed to the letter – doing so
would eliminate two vital elements in the methodology: spontaneity,
and your own musical skills. It's a basic tenet of creative workshops that
participants/students should feel that they co-construct the material. This
applies equally to the music leader/facilitator. Use your creativity, and
awareness of the participants' abilities, to shape the process. Treat the
instructions as a framework, not a recipe.

There are some important principles inherent in this methodology that
may make demands upon you as a musician and music leader: ensembles

GUIDE TO CLASSROOM WORKSHOPPING

should consist of the instruments that the participants bring or enjoy playing, meaning that the ensemble is unlikely to resemble any standard instrumental group; use of notation should be seen as an independently chosen aide-memoire, not a pre-requisite for taking part; and musical starting points should be open so that participants can contribute their own compositional ideas to the final piece. The trade-off for these additional challenges will be the sense of freedom, ownership and creativity that this process should engender among your students.

Freedom, however, should not be equated with 'anything goes'. Your students need to understand that even basic exercises need to be performed *musically* and with precision, and that generating musical ideas requires re-working and refining, not endless repetition of the first thing that comes to mind.

By its very nature, this work encourages creativity and experimentation that often results in the music evolving and developing in new and unexpected directions. If a workshop is functioning well, this is precisely what should happen and ultimately is what you should aim for. Be prepared to follow the creativity of your sessions, to change, develop and discard anything that is written here, and to devise and create projects that are unique to your students.

TEACHING/FACILITATING STYLE

If you're new to facilitating large-group music-making, we hope that the two mini projects introduced here will be sufficiently detailed to give you a solid start. It's a way of working which can provide opportunities to genuinely personalise each session of music-making. Participants can make an important contribution, within their competence levels. Don't expect miracles: the first few completed pieces will not resemble typical 'orchestral' scores, and they will inevitably reflect your students' personalities. But, if you consistently create a shared, open and democratic musical environment we believe you will see increased motivation and enjoyment levels among your students. If, after trying out these materials, you re-visit the original CONNECT films (see **www.musicalfutures.org.uk/ classroom+workshopping**) you'll see that such approaches can result in subtle and sophisticated group performances.

The music will work most successfully if you allow it to develop its own character according to the make-up of the group. This material is merely a starting point that gets a group playing and listening. As you gain confidence in the process and in your students, be prepared to pick up on ideas they have, or intricacies in the way they play, and use that to inform the music.

Some tips for teacher/practitioners leading creative group composition:

- Instill confidence among your students from the outset by giving positive feedback – this way of working may be new to them, especially improvising in front of their classmates

- Don't be afraid of playing yourself – it can help to clarify what you're saying, and students like hearing something that impresses them. Be practical in your method of teaching, refining and nurturing the music

GUIDE TO CLASSROOM WORKSHOPPING

- Keep students in their comfort zones during the first session/sessions and gradually move them out, so that that they feel challenged but at a level with which they are comfortable

- Don't worry as things get messy. This music is all about the groove. If the rhythm section is tight, you can have the luxury of chaos over the top of it in the knowledge that at anytime you can count everyone out except the rhythm section. Over time, students will learn to listen better and lock in with the groove

- Find ways of tapping into the repertoire of music the students are already familiar with

- So many interesting things happen by accident – allow mistakes and build from them

- The sessions won't always evolve at the speed you expect. Sometimes you may need to do more or less than you planned for in a session, so always have some back-up ideas

- Give boundaries within which students can make their own decisions and contributions to the music. For example: 'Can you use these four notes and come up with a short melody?' or 'Do you want to play A or B – which do you think sounds better?'

- Make sure that you balance talking and doing: allow plenty of time for playing and punctuate it with a few focused, inspiring and insightful points

- Develop a conducting repertoire and technique. A few visual cues can indicate a wealth of information

INTEGRATING THE MATERIAL INTO YOUR PRACTICE

The two mini projects explore the initial stages of facilitating group composition. This process should work for practitioners relatively inexperienced at leading creative ensembles. Each project begins with non-instrumental warm-ups that prepare students for listening, improvising, composing, arranging and performing activities. The projects demonstrate how small musical ideas can be developed into complete compositions.

The accompanying DVD (which is also available on the website to download at **www.musicalfutures.org.uk/classroom+workshopping**) illustrates in practice most of the processes outlined below. We recommend that you watch relevant DVD clips, as indicated in the text, as you are reading through the material. It takes you through all of Project 1 in detail (Project 1 particularly is designed for beginners to this approach), and Project 2 shows you some slightly more creative and challenging ideas. Tim Steiner is the project leader in this film, as well as being the author of these materials. He worked with a group of mixed-ability Year eight and 9 students from Morpeth Secondary School, Tower Hamlets during the recording of these clips. You will notice that the group is about half-the size of a 'normal' class, this approach works just as well with larger classes although it can sometimes be helpful to have the support of an additional music leader (peripatetic teacher, older student, etc).

GUIDE TO CLASSROOM WORKSHOPPING

NOTATION

Notation has been used throughout the materials to explain musical ideas. These are intended for your use only and should not be used with the students.

TECHNOLOGY

Using technology within live, creative group sessions can be challenging and it is important to set clear and achievable challenges for students working with computers. The most straightforward method is to use a computer as a synthesiser that can be played via a keyboard. A more complex process could involve programming the core groove of a project and using this as part of the rhythm section. Alternatively, textural soundscapes developed independently on computers can be played to create alternative sections of a project, or as a colouristic textural part of a groove. Also NUMU (**www.numu.org.uk**) is a useful resource for storing recordings (audio and video) of each lesson in its 'Projects' facility.

OPTIONAL OUT-OF-HOURS LINK

These projects could form starting points for developing out-of-hours 'creative ensembles', made up of students of different ages, abilities and with varying musical backgrounds and interests. As part of their Approaches to Personalising Extra-Curricular Learning the Leeds pathfinders developed a model for 'all-comers' ensembles. See the *Breaking the Mould* resources on **www.musicalfutures.org.uk/classroom+workshopping**

Project 1: Groove, Head and Solos

NON-INSTRUMENT WARM-UPS AND PREPARATION

Before starting arrange the group in a circle without instruments.

WARM-UP PART 1

💿 **DVD Project 1 Track 1**

- One student plays a steady beat on a cowbell throughout the exercise
- One by one, indicate to each student to begin clapping a steady beat, until all the students are clapping a steady beat together
- Following a count of four students clap any rhythm they like
- Following another count of four students switch back to clapping a steady beat
- When this process is working well, experiment by cueing different groupings of students to clap rhythms, while others clap the pulse

WARM-UP PART 2

💿 **DVD Project 1 Track 2**

- One student plays a steady beat on a cowbell (or similar) throughout the exercise
- One by one, indicate to each student to begin clapping a looping rhythm over the beat. This process continues until all students have been brought in
- Point to a small group of students indicating to them that following the next count, they should continue to loop their rhythm while everyone else stops
- Following a few bars of the small group playing, count everyone else back in again
- Continue this process experimenting with differing small group combinations

> **TIPS**
>
> - If you are limited for space in your classroom, you will need to find a way to arrange everyone so that most people can see most other people. At the very least, everyone needs to be able to see you and you need to be able to easily point to individuals or groups. If keyboards are facing the wall arrange them so that players can sit behind them and see you without needing to turn their heads
> - If you don't have a cowbell, a woodblock works just as well. The important thing is that everyone can clearly hear the pulse, and that it can be played competently

GUIDE TO CLASSROOM WORKSHOPPING

INSTRUMENTAL WORK

Arrange the group in a circle with instruments. This project works best with a mixture of tuned and un-tuned instruments together with voices. If students already play an instrument, it can be good for them to play it here. However, they may also benefit from trying something new. In the following exercises, you can regularly ask the group to swap instruments in the early stages. You only need to fix them when you start to pin down material.

> **TIPS**
>
> ○ If a student refuses to play an instrument, this can be the result of a lack of confidence. If this is the case, let the student sit and watch for a while. Look for an opportunity to encourage that student to play – for example, a moment in which the class really needs someone to strike a cymbal, and there is no one to do it
>
> ○ If you have an issue with everyone wanting to play the same instrument (for example drums), consider leaving them out initially, and then gradually introduce them to key individuals later on

RIFF WORK PART 1

DVD Project 1 Track 3

The process for this exercise is the same as for Warm-up Part 1 but with the students now playing instruments. Tuned players should use the pitch D at any register. Guitarists should use the chord Dm.
Un-tuned players can use any sounds.

○ One student plays a steady beat on a cowbell

○ One by one, indicate to each student to begin playing a steady beat along with the cowbell:

ALL PLAY D ON THE BEAT

○ Continue the process until all students are playing

○ Following a count of four the students should play any rhythm they like

○ Following another count of four the students switch back to playing the beat

RIFF WORK PART 2

 DVD Project 1 Track 4

The process for this exercise is the same as for Warm-up Part 2, but with students now playing instruments. Tuned players should use only the pitch D at any register. Guitarists should use only the chord Dm. Un-tuned players can use any sounds.

Exercise A: Improvised rhythms on D

- One student plays a steady beat on a cowbell
- One by one, the leader indicates to each student to add a looping phase played in time with the pulse

IMPROVISED RHYTHMS ON D (CUE 1)

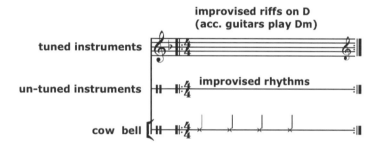

- Continue this process until everyone is playing
- Work through this exercise a few times giving your students advice about what characteristics a good riff might need within this context. Encourage experimentation and listening. By the end of the work, you should aim to have created a strong groove

The following are some examples of simple riffs on D that might be used:

GUIDE TO CLASSROOM WORKSHOPPING

Exercise B: Conducted tutti and solos/groups

 DVD Project 1 Track 4

- With the class playing the groove made in Exercise A, point to one or more players indicating that after the next count, they should continue to loop their riff while everyone else stops. Following a count of four, everyone stops playing with the exception of the selected players. Look for good combinations of 2, 3, 4 or 5 participants to continue looping their riff

- Following a few bars of playing by the selected group, cue the rest of the group back in with a count of four

- Continue this process experimenting with differing soloists or small group combinations

Exercise C: Composed/arranged riffs

In order to develop the music from the basic improvised version above, begin to make decisions with your students about the riffs they are creating. It might be useful to group students playing similar instruments together so they can share their ideas and come up with a shared riff. Take time with this process and listen out for strong ideas. Be prepared to suggest changes to riffs and arrange them for the best overall effect. By the end of this process you should have a clear, strong musical groove.

Assign this groove the cue **ONE**. As the project develops, Cue 1 indicates to players that they should play the riffs developed in this exercise.

FAQS: RIFF WORK

By the time five or six players have joined in, the groove becomes very full and it is difficult to hear the beat

Players often overcomplicate riffs and fail to leave space. Encourage good listening and creative playing. Players must listen to the whole texture and should pay attention to the beat. Don't be afraid to keep a groove going the first few times even if it is a bit messy. It may take time to settle down.

The riffs are all a bit 'samey'

Discuss with your students what makes a good riff. Encourage them to include the use of space, and sustained as well as short notes. Some examples of contrasting riffs are given in the musical example on page 53.

Almost all of the group end up playing the same rhythm

This commonly happens in clapping and playing exercises. Encourage your players to invent individual patterns. Give them ideas of patterns with lots of space. Challenge them to create riffs that are different to the people next to them.

When everyone is playing any sense of regular beat is lost

When students first play in large groups, they tend only to listen to themselves. Encourage good listening, especially to the beat. You can even tell them to listen only to the beat, and not to themselves. Start and stop your groove while keeping the beat playing. Focus on beginnings and endings. Work towards a feeling that the class is playing as part of a large band. Eventually, it should fall into place.

When everyone is playing the groove gradually gets faster

Expect this to happen! Start and stop your groove many times while keeping the beat playing and encourage good listening. If the core beat-keeper speeds up, stop them playing and count them in again at the correct tempo.

There is one participant who just can't play in time

Be tactical with the instruments. Don't consistently give a cowbell to a player who may be challenged in a rhythmic context. Pair up your stronger players with the weaker ones and encourage them to help and lead those who are struggling. You may also consider assigning punctuating roles to players. A cymbal crash once every 32 (or so) beats can really enliven a groove.

The whole thing is really loud and it is difficult to tell what's going on

Expect things to get loud and be prepared to embrace the volume. What on the surface may sound like chaos, can be the result of 30 people working hard on their own part in their own time.

How can I get the group to play more quietly?

Use big contrasts in dynamics. Contrast the instruction 'as loud as possible' with 'as quiet as possible'. Get used to using your hands and arms to control dynamics while a groove is being played.

REFINE THE RHYTHM SECTION (CUE THUMB)

 DVD Project 1 Track 5

Select a group that will act as the core rhythm section. This should be a combination of tuned and un-tuned instruments (for example drum kit/ hand drums, bass guitar, keyboard, guitar).

Listen to the combinations of your players and form the rhythm section by selecting a group of four or five students who are playing strong underpinning parts. If necessary, suggest changes or developments to their parts in order to refine the rhythm section. It is essential that this group can confidently play the groove. An example of the sort of thing to aim for is:

EXAMPLE OF SIMPLE RHYTHM SECTION

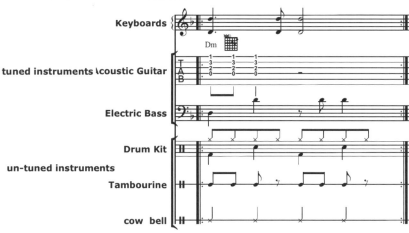

GUIDE TO CLASSROOM WORKSHOPPING

The rhythm section is the heart of the music and will underpin much of the work later on so it is important to get this team working well together.

- Rehearse the rhythm section so they can reliably start playing together after a count of four

- Rehearse cuing in and out other riffs over the rhythm section

- Assign the rhythm section the cue thumb. This means as the project develops, the cue thumb indicates to players that following the next count, only the rhythm section plays

> **TIPS**
>
> - Use a combination of players and personalities in your rhythm section. At its core, you need one or two reliable rhythmic players to hold the groove down. A combination of a kit player or hand percussion player, with a bass guitarist, piano player or guitarist is ideal. If you don't have this, you can ground everything with a cowbell and tambourine
>
> - If your rhythm section sounds shaky and unreliable, experiment with different players and instruments. If you regularly ask players to change what they are doing, they will get used to change. It can be useful to discuss with your group what the rhythm section needs

TEACH THE HEAD (CUE HEAD)

DVD Project 1 Track 6

- Teach the notes of the melody one by one

- Indicate to all the tuned players to play a D as a drone or tremolo

  note 1: D

- Work sequentially through the remaining notes, 2–5.

  note 2: E

  note 3: F

  note 4: G

  note 5: A

The melody works simply with four beats per note gradually rising and descending through the scale. It is likely that as you teach these notes, at least one student will naturally begin playing the scale. This is then easily developed into the melody

- Select a volunteer to demonstrate the melody:

GUIDE TO CLASSROOM WORKSHOPPING

TEACH ALTERNATIVE SIMPLIFIED PARTS TO TUNED PLAYERS IF NECESSARY

- Ask the group to play the melody together. Allow it to be rough and ready at this stage. Allow students to give each other help

- Rehearse small sections playing the melody over a beat

Assign the melody the cue **Head**. As the project develops, the cue **Head** indicates to players that following the next count, the head should be played.

At this stage, you may hear a student playing the melody in a different way, or with some incorrect notes. However, it might sound better the way they are playing! Be prepared for the possibility that you might drop the original version for the newly-created one.

> **TIPS**
>
> - If only a few of the players have tuned instruments you can send a small group of tuned players off to work on the head by themselves. If appropriate, assign one player to lead the group. This is especially good if you have a player who is learning an instrument or who learns very quickly
>
> - Missing notes on tuned instruments are easily accommodated by adapting the melody to the notes that are available

ARRANGE THE HEAD OVER THE RHYTHM SECTION

 **DVD** Project 1 Track 7

Clarify the cues for the group:

Cue **ONE** – Riffs on D, percussion riffs

Cue **Head** – Melody

Cue **Thumb** – Rhythm section players only

- Indicate that the rhythm section is to be played by giving a Thumb cue

- Cue in the rhythm section with a count of four

- Indicate the head is to be played by pointing to your head

GUIDE TO CLASSROOM WORKSHOPPING

- Cue the playing of the head with a count of four

- Experiment with different combinations of instruments playing the head. For example, the rhythm section begins to play. The leader cues in a single player on the head. Following one repetition, more players are brought in. Eventually, all the players are in

ARRANGE THE HEAD OVER THE RHYTHM SECTION

1. cue in the rhythm section
2. cue in the head
3. experiment by cueing in different groupings of head players

Rehearsing the head should be one of the most inspiring parts of the workshop. Use this as a way to rehearse the entire group. Set the rhythm section going and then explore different combinations of instruments playing the head. Experiment with contrasting dynamics and dramatic changes in texture.

SOLOS (CUE 2)

 DVD Project 1 Track 8

- Explain the process of solos to the group. A solo is made up of the notes of the melody, in any order, with any rhythm

- Set up the music so that everyone plays for four bars, followed by cowbell only for four bars:

GROOVE AND SOLOS

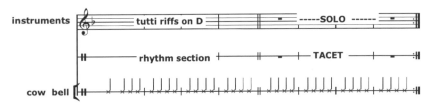

- Once this is established stop the groove and give the group time to practice solos in their own time. Solos should last four bars. Students may choose either to compose their solo, or prepare to improvise their solo. Reassure students that they can bring in some other notes if they like, or make a solo that is 'sound-based'. The important thing is that each student comes up with something, and that they begin to be creative and confident with their ideas

- Set up the groove and indicate soloists play during the four-bar breaks

- Assign solos the cue **TWO**. This means as the project develops, the cue **TWO** indicates to players that following the next count, the cued player should play a solo

FAQS: SOLOS

The solos are tentative and timid. How can I get soloists to play more confidently?

Allow time to practise all together with solos. Set the rhythm section and let the group practise as a whole. Gradually, pair things down to small groups or individuals playing solos. Let solos be short and have pauses.

Do the solos have to be improvised?

No. You can set an assignment for soloists to compose their solos.

Do the students need to stick to the notes of the mode?

No, they should be used as a starting point. Students should be encouraged to explore and experiment.

REHEARSE THE MATERIAL AND CUES

 DVD Project 1 Track 9

The group should have now developed music to four cues:

Cue **Thumb** – Rhythm section players only

Cue **ONE** – Riffs on D, percussion riffs

Cue **TWO** – Solo

Cue **Head** – Melody

- Rehearse each cue by showing the cue, and then counting the group in and out
- Rehearse switching from cue **ONE** to cue **Head**
- Experiment by cueing different combinations of players
- Rehearse building cues gradually
- Use the core rhythm section players to underpin everything. If parts slip out of time, strip the texture back to the rhythm section and count the other players in again. This process should be a creative and energetic playing and exploration of material. Don't worry about things not sounding right yet. Allow the students to play and get comfortable with their material. Over time, students will start to feel the groove and begin to listen to things as a whole. This process cannot be rushed! Allow time and roughness in the process. Get a good feel about the sound, strengths and weaknesses of the group

ARRANGE A STRUCTURE (FIXED)

 DVD Project 1 Track 10

- Discuss an order of events with the class. Write this on the board
- Try out the structure and discuss it further with the students
- Be prepared to modify things and try out ideas even if you don't think they will work
- Try out the modifications

GUIDE TO CLASSROOM WORKSHOPPING

ARRANGE A STRUCTURE (CONDUCTED)

 DVD Project 1 Track 11

As an alternative way to create a performance, use the cues as a way of conducting an improvised structure.

Give clear cues to the players as individuals, small sections and tutti to shape the music as you go.

This process allows for a more responsive and dynamic performance. If a section of the music is going particularly well, you can let it run for longer. If a section fails to work well, you can easily take players out and bring others in.

FINISHING THE PROJECT

Real excitement with this process of music making can happen at the end of a project. Therefore it is always good to arrange a performance. This can be very informal, for example to another class, or even a couple of other teachers. Any audience will give the group a sense of purpose and achievement, as well as having a real focusing effect on a group. Equally, an opportunity to make a recording or a video is also good. This can be done very simply and gives another context for a focused performance combined with an opportunity for listening and appraisal.

Project 2: Groove with Devised Parts, Head, Fills and Solos

This project allows for more creativity and experimentation from the group than Project 1. It is highly probable that students will come up with ideas that are surprising and outside the limits of this project. Take these ideas on board and be prepared to try some of them out. The project is merely a starting point to loosen the creative juices of a class. It is a beginning rather than an end.

NON-INSTRUMENTAL WARM-UPS AND PREPARATION

WARM UP 1: BODY RHYTHM

DVD Project 2 Track 1

- Arrange the group in a circle without instruments
- One student plays a steady beat on a cowbell throughout the exercise
- Gradually teach a body-rhythm such as the following:

Start this on your own and ask the students to join in. Begin with just the chest slap, then the hand-claps, and finally add the thigh-slaps. If necessary, slow the process down and mark the moves through with the class before performing it at speed

- When the students are reasonably comfortable with the body-rhythm, instruct them to play the chest only. Following this, switch to claps only, and then thighs only
- Keep working through until the group has established a confident feel for the body-rhythm

GUIDE TO CLASSROOM WORKSHOPPING

> **TIPS**
>
> - Try to fill the silent beat with a vocal 'HEY!' or a finger-click if the students struggle with the silent 3rd beat. This should help students to understand the structure and to 'feel' it better. You can then lose the 'HEY!' or finger click to reveal the beat of silence
>
> - Body rhythms aren't for everyone. Some of the world's finest musicians struggle to perform a body-rhythm. Therefore if you have students that struggle with this, they may excel with the vocal version below

WARM-UP 2: EXPLORING THE RHYTHM

DVD Project 2 Track 2

Having learnt the body-rhythm, try clapping the entire pattern with the class. Then, turn it into a rap or chant, for example:

voice: You can't help what i'm say-ing if you don't stop me play-ing

Ask the students for ideas for words that could work with the rhythm. Try drawing on ideas for words from the whole group. The ultimate aim is to develop a natural feel for the rhythm.

Some students respond well to working with words, some to working with the body, some to neither. The aim of warm-ups such as these is to offer a range of ways into learning and feeling a rhythm. If one technique doesn't work, it is important to find an alternative.

BUILDING THE GROOVE

DVD Project 2 Track 3

Each student plays a tuned or un-tuned instrument, or works as a vocalist.

- Arrange the group in a circle with instruments

- Ask the un-tuned percussionists to find a way to play a version of the body-rhythm on their instrument. Either set this a solo task, or pair students together. Give them a minute or two to work and then have each one perform their realisation to the rest of the group

- Work to help the students refine their parts. It may work well to combine the ideas of two or three players. Look and listen for strong, complimentary patterns. If appropriate, suggest some modifications or even ask for new parts to be created. Don't be afraid to ask students to learn patterns created by other students and then for those students to play as a section. If students are struggling to find a pattern or play with the right feel, refer them back to the body-rhythm and the chants that were created around it. Some examples of the kind of complimentary patterns that could work are:

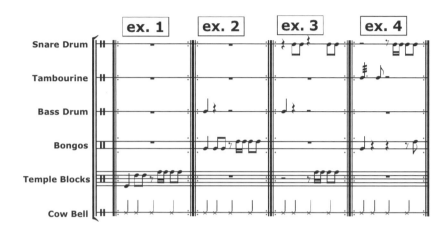

DEVELOPING THE GROOVE

DVD Project 2 Track 4

As the percussion groove begins to emerge, start to build tuned parts.

○ Begin by teaching the following mode to the tuned players and singers:

tuned instruments

GUIDE TO CLASSROOM WORKSHOPPING

○ As a starting point for bassists, show them the following bass line while giving them the freedom to develop the part and make it their own:

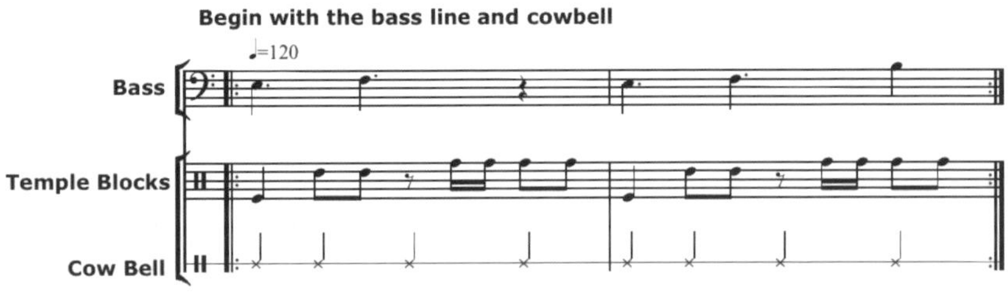

Begin with the bass line and cowbell

○ Begin to establish the core rhythm section with the bass combined with key percussion parts and any core guitars or keyboards

○ Gradually instruct other players to add parts to the groove

○ Assign this groove the cue **ONE**. As the project develops, the cue **ONE** indicates to players that they should play the riffs developed in this exercise

At this stage, the session should be quite messy. This is important. Allow students time to find their own parts and to try things out. As long as you are confident that they know what is required and that you're looking for clear, useful musical patterns the mess and noise is fine. Some students will work very comfortably in this way, but others may struggle. Use your strong students to help out the weaker ones.

When the majority of the class has developed parts, cue in the rhythm section and begin to conduct students in and out of the groove. This is a good stage to invite 'guest conductors' to direct the class. Some students relish the opportunity to direct others in this context, and this can really help to focus the class and the music.

GUIDE TO CLASSROOM WORKSHOPPING

Throughout the work on this groove, you are aiming to develop a feel that draws on the individual ideas of the group, but which works well as a whole. The sorts of things that might emerge are:

EXAMPLE OF GROOVE WITH PARTS (CUE 1)

DVD Project 1 Track 4 shows the group having just developed some parts. The groove is still a little untidy but it works because the rhythm section is already fairly tight.

FAQS: DEVELOPING THE GROOVE

I have no bass instruments.

If you have a few keyboard players, assign them different roles with some playing a bass sound, others piano sound, string sound, organ sound, etc. If you have a piano, use a player dedicated to the lower registers working as a bassist. If you have bass bars, or large xylophones, include these as bass instruments. If you have a few electric guitarists, allocate a couple to play bottom string riffs.

There is a lot of noise and it is difficult to hear what is going on. How can I make it work?

- Bring in your strongest players first. Allow them to establish the feel. This will make it much easier for others to find a way in

- Encourage your drummers and electric guitarists to play quietly

- Embrace moments of chaotic 'working-out'. Expect things not to sound great at first. It will take time for the groove to settle down

- If things are not falling into place, teach participants parts they can play and that you know will work

Should the singers use words?

Words can really help the singers. Either give them a lyric, suggest a theme, or leave it free for them to come up with their own ideas. However, take care that they do not spend all their time writing words – get a couple of phrases sorted quickly. The rest can be developed later.

Should I include MCs with the singers?

No, MCs should work out their own words and develop their own style.

This process is too sophisticated for my group. Can I simplify it?

As with any of the steps, if something doesn't work, simplify it, take a step back, or put the instruments down and do a warm-up or non-instrumental exercise that helps develop any skills that are lacking.

You could consider using the initial processes from Project 1, but instead using the notes and core rhythm of Project 2.

Some of the participants are playing notes that are not in the mode. Does this matter?

The notes of this mode give the piece a certain musical flavour. But they just provide a starting point which can be developed in many ways.

The bass player keeps playing a different rhythm

The body rhythm that begins this project is a starting point. The bass player may come up with something that is more interesting or that works better for their style of playing. Be prepared to go with it as long as it does not undermine the rest of the music.

I have 30 different parts which are all individually good but which don't really work well together.

It is good to draw ideas together. For example, if you have three or four djembe players, encourage them to share their ideas and to develop a part that they all play together.

REFINE THE RHYTHM SECTION (CUE THUMB)

If the groove is not yet flowing, spend time focusing on the rhythm section. As in all groove music, the rhythm section is the key. If the rhythm section works well, it makes it easy to create parts, solos and melodies over it. However, if the rhythm section is not secure, it makes everything else extremely difficult.

- Choose a group that will confidently and reliably act as the core rhythm section. Typically this will be a combination of core accompanying tuned and un-tuned instruments, for example drum kit/hand drums, bass guitar, keyboard, guitar. Refine it as much as you need for it to really work. Experiment with different combinations of instruments and personnel

- Rehearse your core rhythm section so they can reliably start playing together after a count of four

- Rehearse cueing in and out other riffs over the rhythm section

- Assign the rhythm section the cue **Thumb**. As the project develops, the cue **Thumb** indicates to players that following the next count, only the rhythm section plays

GUIDE TO CLASSROOM WORKSHOPPING

DEVISING A HEAD (CUE HEAD)

DVD Project 2 Track 5, 6 and 7

- Teach the tuned group and singers the following phrase:

- Divide the group into pairs or groups and ask them to create a second phrase to fill bars 3 and four. Explain that you would like them to come up with a killer second phrase to the first two bars of the melody

- Ask each group to perform their newly-created phrase

- Discuss with the class which of the new phrases are the most effective

- Choose one or two of the most effective phrases and begin to build a longer phrase. This might be a combination of two or three phrases. The aim is to produce a long melody that everyone will ultimately learn. In DVD Track 6, the keyboard player creates a clear and strong answering phrase that ultimately gets taught to the whole group. The following shows how a longer melody might be created by the use of three newly devised phrases:

- Teach this newly-created head to all the tuned players

- Rehearse the head over the rhythm section and parts from cue

FAQS: DEVISING THE HEAD

What happens if the groups fail to come up with a useful phrase?

Give them some examples, such as those above. Often, participants will feel they need to create something complex. Show them that simple is good. Give examples that use only one or two notes, or which end on notes other than E or B.

What happens if the groups still fail to come up with a useful phrase?

Take fragments of one or two of their ideas and piece them together to make a new answering phrase. A fragment may even be a couple of notes with a simple rhythm.

I have lots of phrases that I want to include. Can I have two or more playing at the same time?

You can do this. However, there is a power of big unison or octave melodies that can be very inspiring and energising. This can really help to contribute to the character and structure of the music you are creating. There is scope elsewhere in the project for layered material so balance this with moments of unison.

SOLOS (CUE 2)

- ○ Explain the process of solos to the group. A solo is made of the notes of the melody, in any order, with any rhythm

- ○ Set up the core rhythm section in a way that allows for soloists to play over it. It might be necessary to thin it out or to coach the players in adjusting their volume according to the needs of the soloist

- ○ Once this is established, stop the groove and give the group time to practise solos in their own time. Solos should last four bars. Students may choose either to compose or improvise their solo. Show them the following notes, but also reassure students that it is fine to bring in some other notes if they like, or to make a solo that is 'sound-based':

The important thing is that each student comes up with something, and that they begin to be creative and confident with their ideas

- ○ Set up the groove and cue soloists to play. Some examples of solos students might aim for are:

If students are stuck for ideas, play some examples to inspire them

- ○ Assign solos the cue **TWO**. As the project develops, the cue **TWO** indicates to players that following the next count, the cued player should play a solo

> **TIPS**
>
> ○ In this context, a solo is a featured part, not a student playing alone. A solo may be improvised or composed. It may be very short and simple. The important thing is that it is an individual taking the limelight, albeit for a short time
>
> ○ If your students are stuck for ideas inspire them with some examples. Demonstrate that solos can be very simple. Play them a solo that for example uses only a couple of notes and/or uses lots of space. Reassure them that their solo might be exactly the same as their riff

CREATE THE B SECTION (CUE 3)

EXERCISE A

○ Arrange the group in a circle without instruments

○ Teach the group the following rhythm loop:

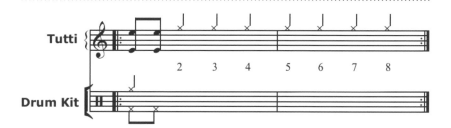

○ Begin with one student playing a steady beat on a cowbell. Start clapping the rhythm yourself before instructing the group to join in. While you are clapping, begin to add the count. Get the group to join in and work to develop a good energy

Leading this exercise without instruments prepares the group for instrumental work. Although it seems very simple, this ensures the students really understand what the groove is. Moving away from instruments also provides a natural break for the ear.

EXERCISE B

○ Arrange the group in a circle with instruments

○ Arrange the section B groove on instruments so that all players play the two quaver beat phrase followed by the count. It may help to double the count on the cowbell or hi-hat (see the example in Exercise A). Loop this groove a few times, gradually working towards a good feel

○ Assign the B section the cue **THREE**. As the project develops, the cue **THREE** indicates to players that following the next count, the group play cue **THREE**

GUIDE TO CLASSROOM WORKSHOPPING

EXERCISE C

- ○ Divide the group into pairs or small groups and ask each to create a phrase to fill the seven-beat break. Tuned players and singers may use any notes. Un-tuned players may use any sounds. They can be as creative as they like with their fills

- ○ When all the groups have created a fill, count the class in to play the basic cue B without fills

- ○ In turn, indicate to a group that they should play the fill in the next seven-beat break by pointing to them. You should end up with a structure similar to the following:

B SECTION WITH FILLS

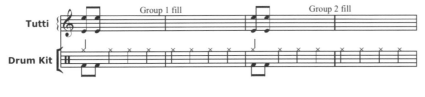

TIPS

- ○ If some of the groups finish more quickly than others, make sure those groups have rehearsed it, and that it is as creative as they can make it. Set them the challenge to make their fill more creative or interesting

- ○ When groups struggle to find anything, give them some ideas to inspire them. Show them a few simple possibilities for their fills that they could choose from

- ○ It can be useful to assign a leader to a group, especially if some of the groups aren't working as well as others. The job of the leader is to ensure that the job gets done

REHEARSE THE MATERIAL AND CUES

The group should now have developed music to five cues:

Cue **Thumb** – Rhythm section players only

Cue **ONE** – Riffs on D, percussion riffs

Cue **TWO** – Solo

Cue **THREE** – B section with fills

Cue **Head** – Melody

- ○ Rehearse each cue by showing the cue, and then counting the group in and out
- ○ Rehearse switching from cue **ONE** to cue **Head**
- ○ Rehearse switching from cue **ONE** to **THREE** to **ONE**
- ○ Experiment by cueing different combinations of players
- ○ Rehearse building cues gradually
- ○ Use the core rhythm section to underpin everything. If parts slip out of time, strip the texture back to the rhythm section and count the other players in again. This process should be a creative and energetic playing and exploration of material. Do not worry about things not sounding right at first. Allow the students to play and get comfortable with their material. Over time, students will start to feel the groove and begin to listen to things as a whole. This process cannot be rushed. Allow time and roughness in the process. Get a good feel about the sound and of the strengths and weaknesses of the group

GUIDE TO CLASSROOM WORKSHOPPING

ARRANGE A STRUCTURE (FIXED)

Discuss an order of events with the class. Write this on the board. For example, you might end up with:

Rhythm Section (RS) x4

RS + Riffs (Cue 1) x4

RS + Head x4

RS + Solo Keyboard x4

RS + Head x4

RS + Solo Piano x2

RS + Head x4

Cue 3 + No Fills x2

Cue 3 + Fill 1

Cue 3 + Fill 2

Cue 3 + Fill 3

Cue B + Fill 4

RS + Head x4

RS + Solo Guitar x2

RS + Head x4

Cue 3 + Conducted Fills

RS + Head x4

○ Rehearse and refine the structure

○ Be prepared to develop and change it. Take time experimenting with the structure. It is likely that students will have strong opinions about this. Try to engage everyone in the decision-making process. Write a few ideas down, and then play them with the class. Assess how well it works, then try an alternative

If it is difficult to remember the structure without looking at the board, you might have made a structure that is either too complex, or very irregular. For example a basic rondo form is much easier to remember than a form which incorporates many irregular shifts.

ARRANGE A STRUCTURE (CONDUCTED)

As with Project 1, an improvised, conducted performance provides a quick and easy way of developing a performance. This kind of performance is energising and allows for the possibility of playing sections for longer (if they are going particularly well), or cutting them off (if they aren't working). You can also play with the structure and the dynamic of the performance. When this is working well, new things can begin to happen.

Remember: be experimental. If things fall apart, you can always bring everyone in for a chaotic tutti moment with everyone playing crazy solos, and then dramatically direct a switch back to the solo rhythm section. The more you play with it, the more fun and more creative it will become.

Make sure your cues are clear and can be seen by everyone, to avoid students missing your cues. If the cues suggested here don't feel comfortable, change them to your own cues. Encourage all of your students to look up. Spend time rehearsing stops and starts without speaking. Eventually the group will focus on the cues.

ARRANGE A STRUCTURE (STUDENT CONDUCTED)

Developing the skills to conduct an improvised structure can take time. Some students will relish this challenge and will quickly learn whether it is the sort of thing they enjoy or not. Having to clearly hold the energy of the entire group and confidently and creatively guide can be a real challenge. It is not always the case that the best players are the best directors or conductors. It is worth spending time allowing students to try conducting. You can always divide the class into smaller teams to play paired-down versions of the music, each with its own mini-rhythm section, parts and conductors.

FINISHING THE PROJECT

As in Project 1, find an opportunity for a performance or performances. By the time your group has worked through the challenges of this project they will have developed a good range of creative and performing skills that will be further enhanced by performances. It might even be possible to give two or more performances. In this case, with each performance, the group's confidence and experience will grow. There will be plenty of opportunity for the group to experiment in each performance and solos can become longer, grooves tighter, and the structure more ambitious.

Following a project of this nature, the group should be ready to fully create its own music drawing on the techniques explored here. It may even be appropriate for the class to split into three or four smaller groups, each with the job of making their own performances.

Whole Class Instrumental Work: Year 7

This section outlines the first project of a programme for Year 7 students developed by Nottingham City Music Service (one of the original Musical Futures pathfinders) and Nottingham City schools, that aims to follow from students' Wider Opportunities experiences (and other musical experiences) in primary schools, and prepare them for Musical Futures work in Years 8, 9 and beyond.

The aims of this programme are:

- To provide appropriate transition and progression into secondary music education for students who have experienced Wider Opportunities in their primary schools, and to accommodate those who haven't

- To provide an appropriate link between Wider Opportunities and Musical Futures, as well as the secondary Key Stage 3 strategy for music

- To meet the requirements of the new Key Stage 3 National Curriculum, delivered in a manner that merges traditional classroom practice with instrumental teaching, and where every student learns/continues to learn a musical instrument

- To reduce the number of instrumentalists giving up shortly after moving to secondary school

NOTE

Watch a film of the Nottingham team running a workshop with teachers about this project at **www.musicalfutures.org. uk/whole+class**

FURTHER READING

The following sites contain information about Wider Opportunities:

www.ks2music.org.uk
(official website for the Key Stage 2 instrumental programme)

www.teachingmusic.org.uk/s/ TeachingMusic/c/Primary
(area where music educators share resources and good practice about Wider Opportunities)

Tuning In – Wider Opportunities in specialist instrumental tuition for pupils in Key Stage 2 (available from **www. musicalfutures.org. uk/whole+class**)

Music Education and the Music Grant: Aspirations, Support and Delivery (DCSF, 2008)

BACKGROUND AND CONTEXT

As mentioned on page 27, one of the most significant developments in primary music education over the last decade has been the success of the Wider Opportunities programme, where every child in Key Stage 2 (KS2) has the chance to learn a musical instrument, free of charge and in normal classroom lesson time.

Wider Opportunities is usually a partnership programme between primary schools and Local Authority Music Services. Music Service staff work with classroom teachers to deliver a programme of practical, whole-class music making. Wider Opportunities is frequently an aural-based approach, with most music initially learned by ear, by copying, and with space for improvisation. The whole-class nature of Wider Opportunities has necessitated the development of new teaching methodologies, many of which have more in common with classroom workshop or African drum circle techniques than traditional instrumental teaching.

Students who have experienced Wider Opportunities are starting to filter through into the secondary sector and, in some cases, are coming into contact with Musical Futures. With Department for Children Schools and Families policy being that all schools will have a Wider Opportunities programme by 2011, one of the traditional music transition problems for secondary schools – the perception that 'they do nothing in primary' – is clearly no longer the case (if indeed it ever was). Therefore, as numbers of students experiencing Wider Opportunities increase, secondary schools are faced with the issue of how to build on the strengths of Wider Opportunities, to support a smooth transition from primary school to secondary school. (See page 28 for what skills and knowledge teachers can expect from students who have been through a Wider Opportunities programme in their primary school.)

RESOURCES

All resources for this project, including backing tracks and optional scores are available from **www.musicalfutures.org. uk/whole+class**

RESOURCES

The project outlined here requires the following resources:

- Alto saxophones, trumpets and double basses (see page 78 for advice on choosing instruments for this project)
- Backing track on CD, CD player plus amplifier powerful enough to be heard while 30 students are playing on top
- Laptop/recorder for audio recording
- Main classroom or rehearsal room, and a number of breakout spaces

WHOLE CLASS INSTRUMENTAL WORK: YEAR 7

INSTRUMENTS

For this programme to work successfully, it is essential that all students have hands-on experience with musical instruments that have credibility outside the classroom. A major factor in choosing which instruments to use is students' prior instrumental experiences. Students arriving in Year 7 are likely to fall into one or more of the following categories:

- They have learned to play a musical instrument as part of a Wider Opportunities programme at Key Stage 2
- They have carried on learning an instrument after the Wider Opportunities programme
- They have learned an instrument through traditional instrumental lessons, either in school, privately, or through informal, self-taught methods
- They have only experienced playing classroom instruments such as percussion or recorder
- They have experienced singing as part of assemblies, classroom activities or a choir

This model makes use of alto saxophones, trumpets and double basses. This combination offers a ready-made ensemble suitable for jazz, Latin and other band models, as well as a wide variety of repertoire and a contextual basis for performance, while also lending itself well to improvisational models. The instruments are immediately appealing and engaging to students from a variety of backgrounds and prior experiences, as well as potentially providing a new but related experience for students who may have learned to play brass, woodwind or string instruments at Key Stage 2.

However, this programme could work well with other instruments. Key factors to consider when choosing instruments are:

- That the instruments used have credibility at Key Stage 3 and make a viable working ensemble
- That where possible you provide links to instruments used in Key Stage 2 Wider Opportunities programmes
- That there are enough instruments for each member of the class to use, with an element of choice involved
- That using guitars, bass guitars and drums is avoided, in order not to pre-empt what might happen in Year 8/9 Musical Futures projects

Students entering Year 7 then have the choice, as part of their music lessons, of:

- Continuing with the instrument they are already learning
- Learning an instrument that is related to the one they experienced at Key Stage 2
- Learning skills on a new (or second instrument)

While there are some advantages to students learning a new instrument – for example students are excited to do something new at secondary school, and it can be easier to plan and manage – there is a danger of falling into the trap of 'starting again' and failing to capitalise on what students have learned at Key Stage 2. In order to recognise this, it is

NOTE
You could use tenor saxophones instead of alto saxophones, which are easier because they are in the same key as the trumpets, but are more expensive, larger/heavier to hold and arguably harder to blow.

important to encourage students to keep playing instruments they have learned at Key Stage 2, perhaps alongside using a new instrument for classroom work, and making sure that the Year 7 programme builds on the generic musical skills that they have already developed. Careful assessment of the best individual route for each student at the start of Year 7 (or at the end of Year 6) is therefore crucial.

IDEAL STAFFING

NOTE

This is a similar staffing model to the Band Instrumental Work project on page 88.

- Three music leaders, one per instrumental group (for example Music Service staff, peripatetic instrumental teachers, teaching assistants, older students or PGCE trainees)

- As this is a hybrid classroom/instrumental teaching model, it is important to ensure that the delivery team has the necessary instrumental expertise across the instruments used

Music Service/instrumental teaching staff might already have experienced teaching Wider Opportunities. If they haven't, it is important to stress the group-teaching methodologies – there is a danger that instrumental teachers without this experience can spend too much time focussing on individual students rather than seeing the bigger picture.

GETTING STARTED

This project is designed to run over six sessions, which could be half a term, or a full term with sessions taking place every fortnight. If the latter, intervening weeks can then involve school music staff exploring aspects of salsa (and other musical traditions with roots in Latin American styles) through activities such as listening, use of keyboards and music technology.

There are some clear benefits to running lessons fortnightly. Students can lose enthusiasm on their instruments if too many lessons stick to exactly the same format, with only the repertoire changing. Running lessons every two weeks can mean that instrumental work doesn't lose its appeal. It also means that there is a variety in the format of the lessons.

WHOLE CLASS INSTRUMENTAL WORK: YEAR 7

CAROUSEL: *TOCA BONITO*

(Sessions 1–3)

The start of this project runs in a similar manner to the band carousel described on page 90.

- Divide students into three groups: saxophone, trumpet and double bass (or three groups of instruments of your choice)
- Students spend one lesson on each instrument (three lessons in total so each student experiences each instrument) in order to:
  - → Develop basic instrumental skills on saxophone, trumpet and double bass
  - → Learn the two notes that they will need to be able to play *Toca Bonito*
  - → Explore the basic features of salsa

At the end of each lesson, all students regroup to perform their parts together against the backing track, in order to experience playing together as an ensemble.

After this carousel of lessons, students choose the instrument they would like to use in class for the rest of the project/year. This is allocated through first/second choices and 'talent spotting' if necessary. It is perfectly feasible for students to opt to use a different instrument they can already play for the rest of the year if they choose.

TOCA BONITO

Toca Bonito is a simple but genuine salsa piece that demonstrates many of the key features of salsa – for example a 3:2 clave pattern, lines in 3rds/6ths, syncopated rhythms in the melody and backing, etc.

LEARNING *TEQUILA*

(Sessions 4–6)

Students will already be familiar with some of the notes in *Tequila*, as they were used in *Toca Bonito*. They now learn how to improvise simple melodic material through call and response and rhythmic word games. Ensemble skills are developed through playing the piece as part of a Latin jazz band and following a conductor.

- As students enter the classroom, music leaders play *Tequila* over the backing track, encouraging the students to join in with the shouted 'Tequila!' at the right times
- Briefly discuss the style of this piece. Identify the swing feel and the way it switches to straight quavers just before the shouts of 'Tequila!'. Discuss the origin of the piece from Latin America. What are the features in common with *Toca Bonito*? What is different?
- Students internalise the melody as a whole group through singing (call and response) then break off into separate rooms with their instrument group (saxophone, trumpet or double bass) to begin learning their part
- Split the melody into two sections to help the students learn their part. You may find developing finger charts and simple stave or graphic notation helpful here
- Students should be able to play the whole melody by the end of the lesson, and give a rough performance as a whole group against the backing track

NOTE

This refers to the version of *Tequila* heard on the backing track, other versions may be different.

WHOLE CLASS INSTRUMENTAL WORK: YEAR 7

The process of learning *Tequila* should be as musical as possible, and the tunes should be learned by ear before introducing any notated versions. Many students will be familiar with this way of working from their primary Wider Opportunities experiences.

A possible structure for these instrumental break-out sessions might be:

- Ask students to sit in a circle with their instruments in an identified rest position

- Lead some call and response work, initially around one note. Any technical work that needs to be done, can be tackled at this point, and should relate to the material. For example, with trumpets, early sessions where students are practising developing their lip muscles by 'buzzing' on mouthpieces can already involve introducing rhythms from the piece

- Teach students a new note and then, to practise that note, use it to learn the rhythm of *Tequila* by call and response. Build up skills with as little talking as possible to keep a musical flow going – learning by watching and copying. Gradually expand the note range until students are playing back the main riff from *Tequila*

- Get a beat going (using a keyboard or music technology drum backing). Go round the circle one at a time and ask each student to play the *Tequila* riff, with a four-beat gap in between (the idea of this is that in future weeks this forms a useful gap for improvisation). You can also do this by starting with one student playing, and adding another student on each repetition, with the aim being to match tone quality and encouraging them to really play together and listen to each other

- Introduce several different notated versions of the main riff – some accurate and others not. Ask students to identify which one is the most accurate. Explain about swing/straight quaver conventions, and ask students to have a go at playing the patterns both straight and swing

- Sing through the second section of *Tequila*, introduce the new notes and put a simple notated version of it on the board. Demonstrate it a couple of times, making sure that students understand that the section just before the 'Tequila' shouts uses straight quavers

- Ask students to practise this second section in pairs for a few minutes, giving guidance to each other, while you go round and help students who may be struggling. It's quite possible that peer leaders will have naturally emerged by now and may help with this informally

- Practise putting the whole tune together over the *Tequila* backing track. Start to think about performing skills – most classes like putting in short movement routines as part of their playing (for example twirling the basses or raising trumpets in the air while shouting 'Tequila')

NOTE
This is helpful in enabling you to identify students who have picked this up easily as well as any who are struggling. There are more challenging parts for *Tequila* that could be used with students who do pick this up quickly.

Shortly before the end of the lesson, bring the three instrumental groups together to show the other groups what they have done and try putting the band together over the backing track. Identify any difficulties that arise (for example getting out of time) and ask students to think about how they can improve this next week.

TECHNOLOGY TIP
Make the backing track available for practice during the week, for example uploaded as a project onto NUMU (www.numu.org.uk).

WHOLE CLASS INSTRUMENTAL WORK: YEAR 7

INTRODUCING IMPROVISATION

Ask students what they understand by 'improvisation' and relate this to their primary Wider Opportunities experiences. Have a staff performance of *Tequila* that includes an improvised section (improvising only on the notes students have learnt). Ask students to think about what the musical characteristics of salsa/Latin jazz are. Draw out some of the things they will need when improvising to fit with the style.

Split students into their instrument groups, and, using call and response:

- Start with one note playing a rhythm over one bar, and then gradually add more notes. Students respond by copying exactly. Begin with straight rhythms then develop more of a syncopated/swing feel. Can students hear the difference between 'straight' and 'swung'? Ask them why/how it is more appropriate for this genre?

- Expand further by calling a phrase and expecting students to respond with an answer, where they are not allowed to copy exactly but should have a 'musical conversation' with you

- Extend these small ideas into longer improvisations, lasting two or four bars, and adding the remaining notes

- Students then spend a few minutes having a musical conversation with each other, checking that they are achieving the right feel for the style

- Remind the group of the main melody with improvised section, following a conductor. Re-group as a whole class to perform *Tequila*, incorporating a selection of their improvised solos

Ask students for their feedback: Did the soloists have a good feel for the style? Did everyone play in time? How could it be improved for next time? Listen to a professional recording of the piece for comparison.

STRUCTURE OF *TEQUILA*

> **4 bars introduction**

> **4 bars – basses only (C, G, C,G)**
> **Tune A (x4) all instruments**
> **Tune B all instruments**

> **Repeat above**

> **Solo section x2 solos**
> **Section B**
> **Solo section x2 solos**
> **Section B**
> **Solo section x2 solos**
> **Section B**

> **4 bars – basses only (C, G, C,G)**
> **Tune A (x4) all instruments**
> **Tune B all instruments**

PERFORMING, EVALUATING, FEEDING BACK

- Begin the final lesson with a staff example of a bad performance. Ask students what was good/bad about it? How can it be improved?

- Using students' ideas give another performance and ask them whether they feel it has improved

- Divide students into their instrumental groups for a final rehearsal and decisions on who will do the solos

- Re-group for a whole class performance, which should be recorded, followed by student and staff feedback

It is important to link the classroom work with performance opportunities – ideally in a variety of in- and out-of-school contexts. Performing in a concert/event within the first few weeks of starting instrumental work can be highly rewarding and motivating for students.

WHOLE CLASS INSTRUMENTAL WORK: YEAR 7

ASSESSMENT

Clear, creative and consistent approaches to assessment should permeate this project. Students should be familiar with the level at which they are working, and be able to explain what they need to do in order to progress in their knowledge, skills and understanding. However, this must not simply be achieved by looking at the final 'summative' performance experience. It is important to take a much more holistic approach, by continually assessing what is going on within the classroom, and using the expertise of all the members of staff through a shared framework.

It is worth noting that the teaching and learning methodology embodied by Wider Opportunities will tend immediately to draw students towards higher National Curriculum levels than more traditional learning experiences. Students are playing individual parts within an ensemble, improvising, developing solos and participating in an ensemble, composing/arranging for, and even conducting contextually-informed performances across a variety of genres and styles. They learn how to make subtle adjustments to their own part to fit with different parts and the conventions of different styles (for example, learning to lock to a clave beat); listen with discrimination and work to improve their performances in the light of those styles. These experiences have a hugely positive impact on students' confidence and self-motivation.

ADAPTING TO SUIT INDIVIDUAL STUDENTS

The Wider Opportunities/Musical Futures programme offers teachers much flexibility when planning how individual students may access the curriculum most appropriately. Some instruments are more instantly playable than others, which may offer the short-term rewards upon which some students with special educational needs thrive. Within each instrumental 'mini-group', there should be a wide range of differentiated performance material available within any given piece of music. Parts can be simplified or elaborated to suit the individual needs of any student, while a variety of notation may be used to support the fundamentally aural teaching framework.

The programme is also easily adapted to Gifted and Talented students, who can access the musical experience at a variety of levels. Several students who already play one of the instruments chosen might elect to choose a new instrument involving different techniques to broaden their skills. These students can have repertoire extended, but might also be used for conducting, arranging and composition work, or to become classroom assistants and peer leaders among their contemporaries. This genuine sense of student leadership can be hugely empowering.

The *Toca Bonito* carousel usually shows if a student is able to play/get a sound from their chosen instrument, and allows them to make an informed choice. If, after this, students begin to struggle near the beginning of the first term then change is possible (though this needs handling sensitively, to avoid a mass exodus to try something else). Alternatively, staff should ensure each piece has a range of more simple and difficult parts to suit different student's ability.

OPTIONAL OUT-OF-HOURS LINK

Consider starting a salsa band for Year 7 students, to enable those who particularly enjoy or excel in this project to continue to develop skills and repertoire outside lesson time.

CASE STUDY:
NOTTINGHAM EMMANUEL SCHOOL

Andy Wolfe, Head of Music at Nottingham Emmanuel School, has been running the Year 7 Wider Opportunities/Musical Futures programme in his school for two years.

❝ There is no doubt that achievement levels in Year 7 have increased rapidly under this curriculum model which facilitates practical musical making so easily and in such a variety of formats. Key to this has been the confidence building that the project offers students, and the relatively instant sense of public success offered by built-in performances.

The school entered into a partnership agreement with the Local Authority Music Service who were able to loan the instruments for the programme free of charge (using the DCSF instrument fund, part of which can be used for transition programmes). This then involved a sliding scale of these costs being met, in order to make the project sustainable within the school. In the first year, all external staffing costs were met by Nottingham City Music Service. The school's contribution will increase over the following two years, before taking the project on entirely thereafter.

In terms of staffing, post-16 students have been involved from the start as classroom assistants. It has been particularly useful when these students are proficient in the given instruments, though not necessary.

Year 7 students have enjoyed the opportunity to take part in the project, most notably the chance to play instruments they might not otherwise encounter. Parents have also been very impressed with the exciting way in which the secondary music curriculum begins and the opportunities it affords their children.

There is variety in learning style within this programme: some music is learnt by ear, some from notation, some pieces are student-composed. Some units are based around music where all learn the piece on their 'main' instruments initially, but some may sing or play drums in the final performance, while some students create the backings for performances using sequencers. In another unit, students create their own accompanying parts for their instruments to a well-known song, and then work with older students who form a backing band, or learn a piece to perform as part of the school play. Changing the instrument groupings works well too, so for some units students work in their own small band with one or two of each instrument. We've worked at keeping it fresh with the genres (including pieces the majority of students know and like).

To some extent, this programme acts as something of a shop window for more traditional instrumental teaching in the school. It can help to keep students playing through the difficult school transition period, and bring back on board those who have lost interest towards the end of primary school. However, it is important for instrumental teachers to be fully aligned with the teaching methodologies of Wider Opportunities if students are to retain their engagement with their instruments through regular group work and performance opportunities.

As a school with a very high proportion of students on the Inclusion Register, we have found only a tiny number who have struggled to access this programme. This is hugely exciting and empowering for students who may have found more traditional teaching methodologies more difficult to access.

Our students have told us: 'In primary we had to play the recorder which was boring, but this is more fun and we got to choose which instrument we wanted to play'; 'None of my friends in other schools get to learn these instruments. They have to do the keyboards all the time. We're lucky'; 'I've played other instruments before but the saxophone's my favourite. I like doing concerts and I've started having lessons on it too.' **"**

COMPLETE PROGRAMME

The project described above forms the first unit of a year-long programme for Year 7 students that can support the transition from Wider Opportunities to Musical Futures. The following table shows how the Nottingham team structures their programme over an entire academic year:

Term	Unit content	End of unit
Half Term 1	**Music and Melody: Carousel** 3 x Week A – Carousel on each instrument working on *Toca Bonito*. 3 x Week B – working on contextual background of salsa etc, composing, arranging and performing backing material for *Toca Bonito*.	Recorded class performance of *Toca Bonito* at the end of the project. Contextual analysis and arrangement of given Salsa material. End of unit: Choice Point for instruments for rest of year.
HT2	**Music and Improvisation** Working on improvisation within the structure of *Tequila* on instruments. Related keyboard improvisation project.	*Tequila* class performance, or end of term performance in public concert. Solo keyboard recording of improvisations.
HT3	**Music and Narrative** Creating own song: composition, instrumentation and performance with emphasis on music and lyrics telling a story. Mixture of singing and instrumental work/cross curricular links to history.	Small group compositions/recorded narrative songs (combination of sung and instruments). Class performance from each group.
HT4	**Music and Notation** Unit looking at thematic analysis of the *James Bond* theme, moving towards staff notation of arrangement.	Class and public performance of *James Bond* to live video. Thematic analysis and notation.
HT5	**Music and Film** Unit giving the opportunity to compose and record film music – combination of live instruments and music technology based project.	Small group composition for a give film scene, where each student records a solo line. Class performance from each group.
HT6	**Music and Theatre (or Music and Genre)** Project based on current school show (or a specific popular song genre) leading towards a large group performance with the accompaniment of an older band from the school.	Recording and performance including singers, older band from the school and instrumentalists (for example *Johnny Be Good; Hallelujah*) Large-scale public performance point.

Band Instrumental Work

This project is designed to equip students with basic instrumental, ensemble and listening skills, as well as an understanding of musical structure and of the learning processes of 'real' musicians. It requires you to establish a carousel of lessons, in which students have one session on each instrument learning the parts of a popular song, and to then 'talent spot' students into bands where they put the instrumental parts together to create their own cover version.

This project is structured into two sections:

- Band carousel sessions

- Band work

The Musical Futures website (**www.musicalfutures.org.uk/band+work**) has the following songs and accompanying resources available to download:

- Coldplay: *Clocks*

- Kaiser Chiefs: *I Predict a Riot*

- Greenday: *Boulevard of Broken Dreams*

We would strongly encourage you to take this concept and adapt it to any song that you feel is appropriate for your students. There are various resources on **www.teachingmusic.org.uk** that teachers have developed themselves for this project.

TECHNOLOGY TIP

Show Me How to Play
(**www.showmehowtoplay.com**) is a multimedia resource that provides numerous songs by current artists, broken down into guitar, bass, drums, keys enabling students to watch the films, isolate their parts and learn them. Schools can download the free 'multiplayer' software, and then pay per download. This is a great tool for students to work with in an informal way. *Show Me How to Play* has kindly donated the audio for Coldplay and the Kaiser Chiefs which you can download for free from **www.musicalfutures.org. uk/band+work**. *GOMIX* (**www.gomix. com**) and *Pure Solo* (**www.puresolo.com**) are also websites that provide broken-down songs/backing tracks for remix/use.

PREPARATION

- Visit the Musical Futures website (**www.musicalfutures.org.uk/ band+work**) and decide upon one set of tracks to download, or break down a song yourself

- Prepare the backing track for rehearsal purposes

- If you are choosing your own song, choose one with a simple structure based on repetition/riffs throughout, ideally using something that is currently in the charts or that your students will definitely know. The advice on choosing appropriate songs for Musical Futures work in the informal learning section on page 149 also applies here

RESOURCES

- At least four practice/rehearsal spaces
- Additional music leader support (two or three music leaders – see below)
- Recording equipment and CD player
- A PA system and vocal microphones
- Any additional resources/worksheets to help students (guitar tab, notation etc), for example resources are available for the above songs from **www.musicalfutures.org.uk/band+work**
- Depending on the size of the class, a selection of the following instruments in roughly equal numbers:
  - → Drum kits and sticks (or electric drum kits/drum machines)
  - → Bass guitars and amps
  - → Electric guitars, plectrums and amps
  - → Keyboards

Depending on the song, other instruments can be used as part of the carousel – for example, violins have been used particularly successfully. Also, students could share instruments such as drum kits – by rotating on drum kits one-between-two (two minutes on, two minutes off for example) or the drum kits could be divided.

This model assumes the class dividing into four groups on a four-week carousel. With a larger class, it may be necessary to expand this to 5 groups over 5 weeks, and having vocals or rhythm guitar as an extra component.

ADDITIONAL SUPPORT

This unit relies on the classroom teacher having some additional music leader support in the classroom, at least for the first part of the unit, so that each group (for example guitars/bass, drums, keyboards) can receive coaching on their instruments. Additional music leader support may be:

- Peripatetic instrumental tutor
- Community musician
- Teaching assistant
- PGCE student
- Other teachers from within the school who have musical skills
- Older students from within the school who have musical skills

In the early part of this project, the music leader acts as an instrumental teacher, albeit with larger numbers than in traditional instrumental lessons. Once the students form into bands, however, the music leader's role changes, becoming more of a mentor or coach (although this part of the project could be run by a classroom teacher on their own, or with less support).

BAND INSTRUMENTAL WORK

Therefore, music leaders helping with this project need to:

○ Understand how to support students in developing their own musical identities

○ Understand when it is appropriate to offer help and when it isn't

If possible, begin this project with a performance of the chosen song by yourself and the music leaders. This enables students to hear a live performance of the song and to have something to work towards. It is essential that staff demonstrate their musicality without showing off and intimidating (or alienating) students. Staff members should also perform a bad version at the end of the carousel, for example playing out of time, not listening, playing wrong notes, etc and ask for student feedback before using their comments to play again properly.

DISCUSSION AND EXPLANATION

Explain to students that:

○ They will have the chance to experience playing all instruments in a band

○ After they have tried playing all of the instruments, they will be asked to opt for a first and second choice of instrument

○ They will be 'talent spotted' in the style of the X-Factor. Students who show most potential on a certain instrument will have more of a chance to play it in the bands. This is an incentive for students to focus during sessions

○ There are health and safety issues (for example setting up an electric guitar and ensuring that no leads are trailing on the floor) and they will be responsible for setting up and looking after their instruments

Have a discussion with students about the song they are going to be learning, for example:

○ What is different/similar about the live version (if you do a live performance) and the recorded version?

○ What instrument(s) can they hear in the song?

○ What style of music is the song?

○ What sort of sounds are used by the various instruments?

○ How is the song structured?

BAND CAROUSEL

Divide students into small groups (depending on your available resources). Students will spend one week on each of: drums, bass, guitar and keyboards (or whatever instrumental groups you have chosen). They will learn the drum pattern, bass line and chord sequence for the chosen song as they go through this carousel.

Each small group will be led by a music leader, who shows students basic instrumental techniques, plus one riff/chord sequence/drum pattern from the cover song.

NOTE
The carousel can work equally well with different instruments, and on a shorter time scale – 30 minutes on each instrument for example.

Music leaders will need to cover the following general and more specific work with each small group of students:

GENERAL

- Ask if students have ever played the instrument (for example guitar, bass, keyboard, drums) before

- Explain about the instrument and its role in a band

- Cover any health and safety issues of setting up the instrument

- Encourage students to play the instrument and explore the sounds it can make

- Play through the chosen riff/drum part as a group, introducing in stages, without the backing track

- When students have mastered the part, encourage students to jam with the backing track

- Even though listening and copying is the main form of learning here, worksheets are available online (www.musicalfutures.org.uk/ band+work) for students to use if necessary

- Make notes on each student so that, once the carousel is complete, you have enough information about students' potential on each instrument

SPECIFIC

Bass guitar

- Explain how to hold the bass guitar in the correct way

- Explain the concept of frets and basic techniques for playing notes

Drums

- Show students how to sit at the kit and hold the sticks properly

- Demonstrate the drum pattern of the song. Students then copy, starting with bass drum and snare beats only then building up to the full pattern

- Develop timing skills

- Introduce the concept of drum fills and encourage improvisation

- Facilitate/demonstrate variations of the basic drum beat for more able students

Guitar

- Explain how to hold the guitar in the correct way, the concept of frets and basic technique for playing notes and chords

- Extension work: play the riff/chords using different figurations and at different dynamic levels

Keys

Most students have experienced playing keyboards in class before and these don't always have the same novelty appeal of drums and guitar. Therefore, stress the importance of the 'keys in a band'.

- Explain the concept of chords and fingering

- Demonstrate four-chord sequence played to simple backing rhythm on keyboard
- Assist students in playing the chord sequence and using appropriate fingering to move smoothly from one chord to the next
- Encourage students to play solos/lead the ensemble by counting in and playing against a backing rhythm
- Encourage students to choose an appropriate timbre for each figuration
- Music leaders may wish to assign different voices on each keyboard in order to differentiate student performances
- Extension work: improvise around the chords using different figurations

At the end of some of these 'band carousel' lessons, encourage one student from each instrumental group to try performing together (for example a bass player performing with a drummer), so that students begin to hear how the parts fit together.

TALENT SPOTTING

Once the carousel is complete, work with your music leaders to put students into bands bearing in mind their first and second choice, and trying to avoid gender stereotypes where possible. Each band will be formed of a drummer, lead guitarist, bass guitarist and keys (or other, depending on the instruments in your carousel). Vocalists tend to emerge naturally from within each band, and it can be more effective to let this happen rather than to allocate one vocalist per band (as this can lead to confrontational situations).

BAND WORK

Divide students into their bands (when the 'talent spotting' is complete) where they will spend time working on producing a complete version of the cover song, with coaching and guidance from the music leaders (although, as mentioned above, extra music leaders at this stage are helpful, not essential, and a classroom teacher on their own could run this part of the project).

Music leaders/classroom teachers will need to cover the following in the sessions:

- Explain their role as 'band coach'
- Assign students to their instruments and remind them how to set up their equipment correctly
- Encourage students to explore their instruments in the form of a free 'jam' as a band
- Help students to learn the main section of the cover song (play CD version first if needed)
- Discuss with the band whether anybody will do the vocals or, alternatively, see if a vocalist emerges as a natural part of the process

○ Assist students in learning their individual parts

○ Explain the importance of teamwork in the band (especially supporting the vocalist, if there is one)

○ Work with students on structure (intros, outros, solos), dynamics and performance style

○ Encourage students to develop leadership skills by taking it in turns to lead the band, count the band in and so on

○ Encourage students to listen to their own parts and how they fit into the song, as well as listen to other people's parts and how they fit in with the rest of the song

○ Encourage students to listen to feedback from their peers and incorporate this into their playing

○ Encourage students to take ownership of the work by developing an identity and name for their band

NOTE

Developing students' integrated listening skills is particularly important, especially an understanding of how to listen to each other in a band.

OPTIONAL OUT-OF-HOURS LINK

After each lesson encourage students to attend an after-school session where they can gain extra instrumental tuition and band rehearsal time.

PERFORMANCES

Encourage students to perform their work in progress to other class members and encourage peer evaluation and positive feedback.

During the final lesson, either video student performances, or get students to perform in their bands in a class concert. Performing with a slightly competitive edge, for example in a year group 'Battle of the Bands' gig, can also provide a powerful incentive for students.

BAND INSTRUMENTAL WORK

PROJECT SNAPSHOT

Lesson	Content
1	• Introduction to and explanation of project *(5 mins)* • Performance of chosen song by music leaders *(10 mins)* • Introduce students to the different instruments *(10 mins)* • Divide students into groups and begin the carousel *(35 mins)*
2	• Listen to song, have a class discussion of the song and recap different instruments *(15 mins)* • Students divide into their groups and begin the carousel (either on drums, keys, guitar, bass guitar) *(45 mins)*
3	• Listen to song and recap different instruments *(5 mins)* • Students move into the second stage of the carousel (either on drums, keys, guitar, bass guitar) *(55 mins)*
4	• Listen to song and recap different instruments *(5 mins)* • Students move into the third stage of the carousel (either on drums, keys, guitar, bass guitar) *(50 mins)* • Brief performance and discussion *(5 mins)*
5	• Listen to song and recap different instruments *(5 mins)* • Students move into the fourth stage of the carousel (either on drums, keys, guitar, bass guitar) *(50 mins)* • Brief performance and discussion *(5 mins)*
6	• Allocate students into bands as a result of 'talent spotting' *(5 mins)* • Students divide into bands and work on putting together their songs, coached by the music leaders. Focus on learning the chorus of the song and recording it *(45 mins)* • Playback one or two recordings and encourage peer evaluation *(10 mins)*
7	• Students divide into bands and work on putting together their songs, coached by the music leaders. Focus on learning the verse of the song, structuring the song, linking the sections into an arrangement and recording it *(50 mins)* • Playback one or two recordings and encourage peer evaluation *(10 mins)*
8	• Students divide into bands and continue to work on putting together their songs, coached by the music leaders. Focus on building the complete song, incorporating intro and outro, and recording the work *(40 mins)* • Have a whole-class evaluation of songs, listen to some of the recordings (or live performances), and offer constructive criticism *(20 mins)*
9/10	• Depending on progress, either have a class session where each band performs to each other, or have one final rehearsal lesson followed by another with band performances. Alternatively, organise a 'Battle of the Bands' contest, either as a class or a year group • Follow with an evaluation of the project

RESOURCES
Some materials developed by our
Musical Futures pathfinder teams on
samba and Bollywood are available
from **www.musicalfutures.org.uk/non-western+music**

Non-Western Music

This project is designed to give students the opportunity to learn non-Western music via aural/oral learning, leading to a performance as a world-music ensemble. Integrating this into Musical Futures work initially came from responses from students wanting to experience 'all kinds of music', and from a desire to create non-Western music projects that provided a 'real' performance opportunity, focusing on genuine performing skills in the chosen musical genre/culture. It also aims for as 'authentic' an experience as is possible, within the confines of a classroom.

The resources here focus on taiko drumming, however we strongly recommend that you consider adapting this approach to other non-Western musical traditions, particularly those that might be relevant to your students. Depending on available resources, this project can focus on any non-Western music genre.

The aim is for students to gain a practical insight into the chosen musical tradition, to enable them to experience performing and participating in a world-music ensemble, and to develop an understanding of the cultural context of the music through performing.

TAIKO DRUMMING

Taiko is an energetic form of music-making, that combines rhythm with vocal shouts and physical movement. It develops rhythmic skills, group work and performance skills. Throughout this project, it is important to ensure that students understand the cultural context of taiko, especially the meaning of Japanese words used in the lessons. The following four principles of taiko can help students to understand the link between the context of music and the way it is performed, and to see the lessons as more than just 'playing drums':

- **Attitude:** personal responsibility, focus on achievement, teamwork

- **Kata:** Aesthetics, body language, ergonomics, fitness. Kata encompasses stance and every move you make while playing – it has as much importance in taiko as the sounds made by the drums

- **Technique:** stick skills, rhythm skills, dynamic expression, ensemble skills

- **Ki:** Unity of body and mind, self-expression, energy and joy. The Japanese word ki comes from the Chinese 'chi'. In taiko, it is thought that ki can be achieved when every player is following the other three principles of taiko – kata, attitude and technique

NON-WESTERN MUSIC

It is important that, through this project, students understand that they can achieve as much through their attitude and body movements as they can through playing rhythms.

The emphasis throughout learning taiko is to do simple things really well, and for any performance to look good as well as sound good.

PREPARATION

- Familiarise yourself with the principles, techniques and rhythms of taiko: **www.youtube.com/taikouk** contains a selection of videos of taiko performances by young people and adults

- Assemble your set of taiko drums (or alternatives, see below) in a circle, with a drum for yourself as part of the circle

- Check drumsticks are not chipped or broken, and will not damage either the drums or players' hands

- Ensure floor is clean and safe for bare feet

NOTE

It is recommended that students have bare feet for taiko drumming, as this helps the taiko stance, although this may be a point of conflict with some students.

RESOURCES

- A set of taiko drums and sticks. For a class of 30, you need 15 drums (one per two students). Alternatively use rubber tyres, large plastic industrial containers, parts of a drum kit or other percussion (for example from a samba kit). Taiko drum sticks ('bachi') can be made from broom handles

- Large space, cleared of furniture, with reasonably high ceilings so there is room for the taiko sticks to be raised high enough without danger of hitting the ceiling/lights

KAGEMUSHA TAIKO

Kagemusha Taiko (**www.taiko.org.uk**) is a performing arts/education company. Their website contains information on drum-making, including how you can make taiko drums cheaply from sewage pipe and tarpaulin, as well as further resources in the 'education' section, for schools wanting to take taiko drumming further than we outline here.

GETTING STARTED

Physical warm ups should take place before any practical work. These are essential because they prepare students for the physical effort of taiko. The physical warm up is done while students count eight beats. The aim is to feel a steady pulse as a group and to relax arms, legs and posture in preparation for the practical work.

Due to the physically demanding nature of taiko, allowances may need to be made for students with health problems or disabilities. For example, students with back or joint problems may struggle with kata and need to find an alternative way to address the drums.

POSTURE AND STICK HOLDING

The basic taiko stance is critical for achieving good kata. Encourage students to:

- Rest on the balls of their feet with their knees bent and left leg slightly in front, feet more than shoulder-width apart

VIDEO LINK

See **www.musicalfutures.org.uk/non-western+music** for a video tutorial demonstrating correct posture.

- Hold their sticks (bachi) between the thumb and first finger with the back of the hand facing upwards. Ensure the fingers are wrapped around the stick, NOT pointing straight down the stick to avoid injury

- Slightly bend the elbows and hold the arms away from the body

- Make a V-shape with the sticks towards the centre of the drum

- Relax shoulders and look ahead rather than staring at the drum

In each lesson, encourage the students to check each others' taiko stance: feet, elbows, shoulders, arms, hands, waist, weight evenly distributed.

SHOUTS

Taiko drumming is vocal, and students should be encouraged to use their voices as much as possible to reinforce the rhythms they are playing. 'So-re' (pronounced 'Soar-Ray') is a basic start command, and typical shouts include 'Soh!' 'Hup!' 'Yo!' 'Sah!'

TEACHING DONGO

Dongo is a taiko base rhythm – a rhythm that underpins a taiko composition.

- Divide the class into two mixed groups of equal number

- Show the first group the Dongo rhythm

- Students initially play five straight beats with the right hand, helping to establish the rule that the right hand always plays 'on the beat'. This applies to all, even left-handed students, because of the visual aspect of the performance. Unless of course the whole group decides to switch hands around

- Gradually work in the Dongo beat with the left hand. Think of the Dongo rhythm as 'One-go-dongo, two-go-dongo' or 'One potato, two potato...'

- Swap the groups over, show the second group the Dongo rhythm, while the other group practises by tapping on their knees

Throughout these exercises, the group not playing the drums should watch and copy by tapping on their knees/making the appropriate movements. This means that, when each group is on the drums, you shouldn't be recapping but moving the group forward.

If students struggle with playing a Dongo beat, they can play straight beats with the right hand only.

TEACHING BIG BEATS

Big Beats are played by bringing the stick down from above the head to strike the drum. A Big Beat is followed by a shout of 'Hup!' during which the player raises the other stick above their head. The stick should be raised from the wrist with a 'painting' motion until the arm and stick are

VIDEO LINK

See www.musicalfutures.org.uk/non-western+music for a video tutorial demonstrating introducing the Dongo rhythm. Also, www.taiko.org.uk/resources has more information and notation for teaching *Shimabayashi* – the piece described here.

VIDEO LINK

See www.musicalfutures.org.uk/non-western+music for a video tutorial demonstrating introducing Big Beats.

NON-WESTERN MUSIC

pointing towards the ceiling. To make it look good – and to avoid students hitting themselves on the head – ensure that all students hold the sticks in a straight line with their arm (rather than flipping back on itself) when pointing at the ceiling. The stick should then be brought down from above the head to strike the drum.

- Divide the class into two mixed groups of equal number
- Show the first group how to play Big Beats
- Practice building up to playing a series of eight Big Beats over the dongo base rhythm that you (or another music leader) play
- Swap the groups over, show the second group the Big Beats, while the other group practises the movements

BIG BEATS OVER DONGO

- Divide the class into two mixed groups of equal number
- Start half of the students playing the Dongo rhythm
- Get the other half of the students playing Big Beats, ensuring that the Big Beats and the Dongo rhythms fit together
- The two halves alternate playing the two patterns for eight beats per pattern (using the cue 'So-re' to indicate the changes)
- Swap the groups over, take the second group through the process, while the other group practices the movements

VIDEO LINK

See www.musicalfutures.org.uk/non-western+music for a video tutorial demonstrating introducing Big Beats over Dongo.

TAIKO: DONGOS AND BIG BEATS

R = Right Hand
L = Left Hand

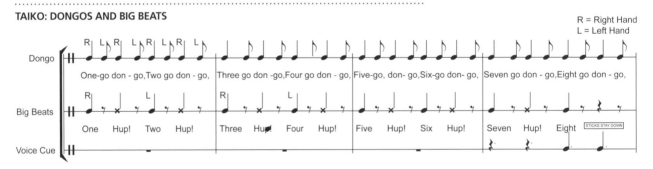

If students have difficulty running Big Beats into Dongos smoothly, pay particular attention to keeping both sticks down after the eighth Big Beat and then starting Dongos with the right hand.

FINISHING LESSONS

Each lesson should end with a formal ritual. The students say to each other 'Otsukare* Samadeshita' ('you are honourably tired, thank you for your hard work') and bow, acknowledging everyone's contribution.

(*Ostukare is pronounced 'Ott-sue-car-ray').

PERFORMANCE

Walking onto stage, addressing the drum, starting and ending the routine, bowing, and leaving the stage are all important parts of the performance process of taiko. Therefore, as part of this project, explore with students a routine for walking onto the stage, or performance area – even if this is just in your classroom – especially towards the end of the project.

ADAPTING TO SUIT INDIVIDUAL STUDENTS

It should be possible for any group of students to perform taiko. If the alternating Big Beats and Dongos are too challenging or if students advance rapidly through this and need more challenge, the following techniques could be employed:

NOTE

Rumbles are drum rolls/tremolo effects played with the sticks. If every player plays a simple right/left beat as fast as they can (with the emphasis on control and lightness of touch rather than speed) a 'rumble' effect is created by the group.

- Investigate dynamics – Dongos or rumbles can be played at five dynamic levels recognised through the height of the sticks above the drum. A gradual crescendo or diminuendo can be an effective introduction to a performance

- Doing work around rituals for addressing the drum at the start of a performance can offer an opportunity to calm and focus a lively group. Students are instructed to follow the leader's movements, allowing the group to step forward and raise sticks over their heads and lower sticks into position in time with each other

- *Dongodon 'So-re' Dongodon 'Sa Sa'* is a simple yet effective rhythm combining beats, movements and shouts:

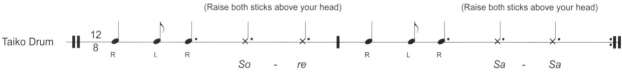

- If students aren't able to alternate Big Beats and Dongos, they could perform Big Beats while a teacher provides the Dongo backing. You could use the verbal instruction 'So-re' to start and stop, rather than requiring students to count their repetitions

- The 'Don Kara' rhythm combines beats with rim shots and increases the challenge of coordinating left and right hands. You play one beat on the skin and then two on the rim, and it can be used instead of Don DoKo (played only on the skin) to create a different sound effect:

Play crosshead notes by striking the side rim of the drum

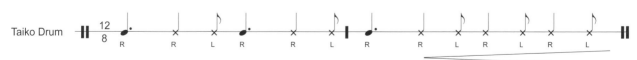

- Taiko can be used to explore improvisation or composition. Students can develop their own rhythms, movements and shouts

- Students can learn to take responsibility for leading the group, either shouting instructions of 'So-re' or leading the movements for addressing the group

NON-WESTERN MUSIC

○ Students can discuss and be involved in the decision-making about the structure of a performance piece

OPTIONAL OUT-OF-HOURS LINK

Scheduling after-school sessions on taiko drumming can allow students the opportunity to spend further time in a group developing taiko skills and repertoire. These sessions aim to lead to the formation of a school ensemble.

PROJECT SNAPSHOT

This project could take between three to six weeks depending on your students, and on whether you just run the basic exercise as outlined above, or whether you source additional taiko rhythms to integrate into the performance. Some teachers even successfully integrate all of the below into one session.

Lesson	Content
1	• Introduction of taiko and its context *(10 mins)* • Warm-up exercises *(5 mins)* • Learn how to hold the sticks, assume the correct posture, and learn how to play Big Beats; perform a series of eight Big Beats, finishing with the sticks down *(40 mins)* • Ritual ending and finish lesson 'Otsukare Samadeshita' *(5 mins)*
2	• Recap on the four key principles of taiko, reminder of holding the sticks, correct stance *(5 mins)* • Warm-up exercises *(5 mins)* • In two alternating groups, one watching and one playing, students learn to play Dongo rhythm; recap Big Beats from previous lesson; combine half of each group playing eight Big Beats with half the group playing Dongo rhythm *(45 mins)* • Ritual ending and finish lesson 'Otsukare Samadeshita' *(5 mins)*
3	• Recap on the four key principles of taiko , reminder of holding the sticks, correct stance *(5 mins)* • Warm-up exercises *(5 mins)* • Practice alternating Big Beats with Dongo rhythms *(15 mins)* • Introduce ideas around performance rituals (walking on, bowing etc) and discuss structure of the piece *(15 mins)* • Each group performs to the other half of the class, with full performance rituals *(10 mins)* • Evaluation *(10 mins)*

SECTION 2: NON-FORMAL TEACHING

Guide to Songwriting

This section provides guidance on how you can support students with songwriting. Songwriting can be an excellent way of enabling students to express themselves about topics that are important to them, and in musical styles and genres with which they are familiar. This guide suggests some processes, techniques and ideas for encouraging your students to write their own songs, without suggesting actual musical or lyrical content – this should come from the students themselves.

All songwriters, whether individuals or groups, write best in their own way, in the order which suits them and their songs, and very often dealing with more than one aspect of the writing at a time – for example, coming up with words and music together. Furthermore, they may well write different songs in different ways. So there is no one way to teach songwriting.

Consequently, there isn't one set way of using this guide. We have suggested a skeleton structure for how you might incorporate this guidance into a six-week project. However, this guide could also be used in a much less formal way, to support students working on composing/songwriting as part of the informal learning model for example (see page 154).

This guide should be treated as a framework – student voice and creativity should form the content and determine the direction of all songwriting work.

PREPARATION

- Either ask students to bring songs to the lesson (for the comparison exercises) or have a number of popular songs of different structures/styles prepared that students can draw upon for discussion and inspiration
- Photocopy the student prompt sheets, if required

GUIDE TO SONGWRITING

RESOURCES

- Practice spaces, one per small group
- Range of instruments – ideally a typical 'band' set up (drums, guitar, bass, keyboards, microphones), and/or acoustic instruments, classroom percussion
- Ideally, access to computers with music sequencing/sampling software for students who want to compose electronically
- Flipchart paper and pens, and if possible audio recording equipment, for students to record their ideas
- Copies of the student prompt sheets, if required

STUDENT PROMPT SHEETS

The following student prompt sheets are available to download from **www.musicalfutures.org.uk/songwriting**:

- Prompt Sheet 1: Adding to our song
- Prompt Sheet 2: Finishing your song
- Prompt Sheet 3: If you just can't get started

Your students may not need to use these prompt sheets and they should be offered as optional guides, rather than fixed instructions.

TEACHING ADVICE

The following set of activities provides a step-by-step guide for how students might start, continue and finish a song. This is not a prescription of how students <u>must</u> write songs, but a series of suggestions and exercises for things they could do, especially if they get stuck.

It is important to stress to students that, when they express themselves in a song, no-one can say that something is right or wrong. However, it is beyond doubt that some songs are better than others and the care used when choosing notes, lyrics, chords, etc, can make the difference between a satisfactory school exercise and a song which is really exceptional.

In this project, we use the word 'write' for making up or creating words and music. This does not necessarily imply writing on paper – and it refers both to the mental activity of creation and the recording of the song. Though some students may prefer to write songs on their own, the material here is written for groups of students writing collaboratively.

LISTENING TO OTHER SONGS

We make specific suggestions for linking listening with songwriting throughout this guide, to encourage students to listen to as many songs as possible.

Students are likely to prefer writing the sorts of songs they enjoy listening to, but encourage them to challenge themselves and write other types of songs as well. Not only will this expand the range of possibilities, but it should improve their overall songwriting style. It also could lead them to discover some new music which they would never have chosen to listen to.

TECHNOLOGY TIP

As listening can guide young songwriters through investigating how others have created great songs, enabling students to have in-school access to online music streaming sites such as Spotify, Last.fm, Deezer and We7 (current sites at time of going to press) can be beneficial.

RECORDING AND REVIEWING

Recording and reviewing work is a critical part of the creative process. It can be particularly frustrating for students if they forget an idea developed in a previous lesson. Flipchart pads and pens should be made available for jotting down ideas and lyrics in progress in whatever way the students choose, and also audio recording devices to record their ideas. These ongoing notes/recordings should be available every lesson.

Recording (either audio or video) is also a crucial way of tracking student progress, both for the teacher and students. It can be very beneficial for each group of students to have a means of jotting down ideas aurally. This could be on their mobile phones (depending on school policy), or other available recording equipment.

COPYRIGHT

It is useful to remind students that, if they are using other artists' words, music or recordings in their songs, they may not be able to play their songs in public or record them for distribution because the material will be protected by copyright. Soundrights (**www.soundrights.co.uk**) is a web-based resource developed by UK Music that provides lesson activities and online resources to help students at Key Stage 3 understand copyright, and how they might need to go about protecting their own material.

WRITING A SONG

'Writing a Song' provides an illustration of the songwriting process, and links the stages to the exercises in this guide.

GUIDE TO SONGWRITING

WRITING A SONG

There isn't just 'one' way of writing a song, or even one 'best' way. The chart below should give you some ideas for how to get started – but you are completely free to go off in your own direction. You can always come back to these suggestions whenever you feel they might be helpful.

Music

- Tunes ⟷ Find chords to fit ⟷ Extend the melody and its chords ⟷ Review, refine your musical ideas

- Chord sequence, riff ⟷ Improvise (Ex. B1) ⟷ Settle on a pattern – add a tune to it

- Think of some words for your music (Go to 'Words') (Ex. B2)

Beginning (Prompt sheet 3)

Words and music

- Grow ideas (Go to 'Words' and 'Music')
- Develop song fragments with words and music

Continuing

- Work on other sections (verses, chorus etc)
- Put together a verse or chorus (Ex. C3/4)
- Consider song structure (Ex. C2, Prompt sheet 1)
- Develop, review, refine your song (Ex. C1, Prompt sheet 1)

Words

- Lyric ideas (Ex. A2) ⟷ Find some rhymes
- Song topic ideas (Ex. A1) ⟷ Write some lines ⟷ Develop, review and refine your lyrics (Ex. A3)
- Begin to discover a tune (Go to 'Music')

Finishing (Prompt sheet 2)

- Record and/or perform the song and listen to what people say about it

SONGWRITING ACTIVITIES

Students often ask whether the words or the music are written first in a song. It may be either, or both together. However, it can be useful to decide before starting what the song is going to be about, which may or may not actually be mentioned in the song.

Students using lyrics as a starting point should work through Exercises A1–A3, and students using music as a starting point should go straight to Exercises B1/B2. If students are beginning with fragments of words and music together (lines for a song) they may use aspects of both methods simultaneously.

Songs don't need to be written in the order in which they are sung/performed when they are finished. In practice, songwriting usually happens as a non-linear process, therefore students should follow the exercises in the order most appropriate to them, and be able to revisit the exercises and refine their work as and when necessary.

STARTING POINT: WORDS

EXERCISE A1: SONG TOPIC IDEAS

Students start by establishing the theme/topic that their song will be based on.

- Ask students to divide into friendship groups, or to work on their own
- Each group should choose a topic on which to write a song and discuss it, writing down or recording any interesting ideas that could be used to inspire their song and its lyrics
- Some of the words and phrases chosen may later be used in the song. But, at this point, encourage students to concentrate on the topic and what arises from it, rather than thinking about the song
- Students should make a note of all of their ideas, and then go through them and decide which ones to use

It is possible that their ideas will be a mixture of words and music or even simply bits of tunes or chord progressions. If the ideas include music, see the B section (page 107).

As part of this exercise, ask students to choose one of their favourite songs, listen to it and discuss what the song is about, for example:

- How many of the lyrics refer to the central theme/topic?
- Do they tell you everything at once or build up a story?
- Is anything else brought in from a different topic; if so, why?

EXERCISE A2: LYRIC IDEAS

After establishing a topic for the song, students now begin writing their lyrics.

- Ask students to review their bank of material for possible lyrics for their song. These needn't be the first lines in a song, although they could be; students are looking for something which fits anywhere in a song

GUIDE TO SONGWRITING

- Where there are verbal phrases, encourage students to find a good rhythmic way of expressing them

- If there are some strong words or phrases, encourage students to search for more words about the topic which rhyme with them and make a list of useful rhyming words

- Students should work on this until they have a few useful sentences and phrases

As part of this exercise ask students to choose one of their favourite songs and:

- Select examples of short phrases – words and music – where these two elements work particularly well together

- Ask them to consider:

  → Why are these so good? Are there any places where the words and music don't fit together well? Does this spoil the song?

  → How are rhymes used – on any words, or on words important to the message? Do the rhymes fit with the rhythmic stresses in any way?

  → Are the words easy to sing: which vowels work well on long notes; which consonants get lost when one word follows another?

- Encourage students to make a phrase of their own modelled on one of these phrases, either by adding their own ideas to what the original song is about, or by choosing another topic for their phrase

EXERCISE A3: DEVELOPING LYRICS AND BRINGING IN MUSIC

Students should now be in a position to develop their lyrics, using some of the material they have developed in Exercise A2.

- Students should spend some time saying aloud, in rhythm, the words they already have written. They should then work on these, adding and taking away words, until they have two lines which work well together as lyrics for a song

- Next, using exactly the same rhyme scheme and rhythm, write another two lines

- If the meaning is not complete, students should continue the pattern (or choose another pattern) to grow the four lines into a longer section

- Students can start to think about how their lyrics might fit to music. If there is no music with the words yet, encourage them to say their phrases in different 'sing-song' ways, gradually singing lines to a new tune

- The second of the two-line groups will usually have new words, but could have the same music as the first two lines. However, students could change the music at the end to make a slightly different second half of the fourth line

As part of this exercise, ask students to choose one of their favourite songs, pick out some two-line phrases and consider:

- Is that structure then repeated immediately afterwards?

- If so, is it changed at all? Is it used again later in the song? How do other two-line phrases – different ones in the same song – relate to the one they chose?

○ Why are things so often expressed in two-line phrases?

○ Encourage students to create a verse or a chorus modelled on the best of these examples, either by adding their own ideas to what the original verse is about, or by choosing another topic

At this stage, it is particularly important to encourage peer feedback, because having another point of view can open students up to writing a song which will be relevant to more listeners. It can also alert students to a songwriting 'habit' which they may use without being aware of it, or warn them of other songs which they may have copied by mistake.

Remind students that the language of song lyrics is different from that of speech, stories, official forms, or even poems. This is because the sound of the words is as important to the message as the meaning. It is also because the songwriter may want to imply more than is being said openly. The music also contributes to the meaning – sometimes the music and the lyrics can give deliberately different messages. Students will need to consider what type of language (vocabulary and grammar) they will be using.

STARTING POINT: MUSIC

EXERCISE B1: IMPROVISING A BACKING

In this exercise, students use jamming and arranging to work up musical ideas for their songs.

○ Ask students to divide into friendship groups, or to work on their own

○ Using instruments and/or voices they should jam around a chord-sequence and rhythm with which they are familiar

○ Encourage students to keep looping their musical ideas until they flow well

○ If students already have an idea for a melody (with or without words), the chords of the backing should fit with it

If the above doesn't work, or as a preparatory exercise, ask students to choose one of their favourite songs and do the following:

○ Play along with the basic accompaniment a few times, and then play their version of the backing without the recording

○ Encourage students to try a few slight changes, for example the order of the chords, the bass line or the feel of the drum beat

○ Practise the new music and continue as above

EXERCISE B2: ADDING A VOCAL AND BRINGING IN WORDS

If there is already an idea for a melody, it could be used as the basis for the next exercises. If not, students should improvise a melody (with or without words) over the backing developed in Exercise B1.

TECHNOLOGY TIP
There are many websites where you can download samples, which may be bass sounds, drum sounds and loops, vocal samples and FX. Students can use these sites to keep their productions sounding fresh and current.

GUIDE TO SONGWRITING

- ⊙ Encourage students to improvise lines of a tune, or to rap verbal phrases in a rhythm which fits their backing

- ⊙ When students have part of a tune which fits the chord progression, they can try putting words or phrases to it

- ⊙ Encourage them to go round this sequence, trying new ideas which work with the backing – they may be able to get more than a single line this way

- ⊙ Once the improvisations bring up some useful lyric ideas consider referring to Exercise A3

The style of an accompaniment can completely change what a song is saying. It can be a good exercise to try out different ways of playing a song to discover the different effects this can have.

PUTTING IT TOGETHER

Students should now have some small sections of a song with words and music. At this stage, the sections may not fit together, but they should feel like part of the same song.

EXERCISE C1: REVIEWING THE MATERIAL

Regularly reviewing and refining music and lyrics is an important ongoing part of the songwriting process.

- ⊙ If the ideas don't really fit together as part of the same song, students could consider which elements could be put aside or changed

- ⊙ As well as coming up with new lyrics ideas, students could try using different words and word orderings to improve the effect of the words that they already have written

- ⊙ As well as practising the music and improving the performance of it, students should be alerted to how small changes can have a powerful effect, and try out different chords and rhythms

As part of this exercise ask students to choose one of their favourite songs and:

- ⊙ Explore how ideas are repeated, developed or replaced in the song

- ⊙ Consider whether any parts of the song don't fit well with the rest of it

- ⊙ Try to write some new words and music which develop these ideas

EXERCISE C2: MOVING ON

Students will potentially have some song material by now, probably still as separate bits. Students can use any structure they like to put this together, however we suggest the basic verse and chorus structure here: **Verse 1, Verse 2, Chorus, Verse 3, Chorus.**

Students should listen to their work and decide whether each completed section or uncompleted idea would work better as part of a verse or part of a chorus.

To help with this exercise, ask students to choose one of their favourite songs and:

- Try splitting it up into different sections, identifying verse(s) and chorus(es)
- Listen to what is 'said' in each part of the song. Do the words in a verse have a different message from another verse, and from the chorus? Is the music different in the introduction?

Now students should try to shape their own material into verses and chorus.

EXERCISE C3: COMPLETING A CHORUS

Students now work to finish their choruses.

- If students already have part of a chorus but don't know how to finish it, encourage them to analyse what they have already got
- Is there anything that still needs to be 'said' in their chorus? Does the music feel complete in itself or is there something missing? If there is still something missing in their chorus, try these suggestions:
  - → Repeat one or two lines in the chorus, or repeat a line with a very slight change (perhaps in the harmony)
  - → Include a line from the verse in the chorus
  - → Check that the students are sure that what they actually have is a chorus. Might it be a different section?

As part of this exercise, ask students to choose one of their favourite songs and analyse the chorus by asking questions such as:

- How long is it, related to the verses?
- Is it in the same key as the verses?
- Does it end with the home key or lead to that?
- Does the rhythmic feel change in it?
- Does it 'represent' the song?

Then encourage students to write their chorus on the same model.

EXERCISE C4: COMPLETING VERSES

Students now work to complete their verses.

- If students already have part of a verse, encourage them to try finishing it off as described in Exercise A3
- When students have finished one verse, they should write a second and perhaps third verse, using the same music and rhyme scheme as the first, but with new words. As far as possible, encourage them to keep the number of syllables in the lines the same, and to be careful where the stresses in the words and sentences fall
- Encourage students to try to move the 'story' of the song on and not simply say the same things again. Students might do this in various ways, for example by telling the next thing that has happened or that they want to happen, or by explaining the first verse further
- If while working on Verse 2 they decide that they want to change the order of the lines or the verses around, that is fine; just because they wrote one verse first, it doesn't mean that it needs to be sung first

GUIDE TO SONGWRITING

As part of this exercise ask students to choose one of their favourite songs and:

- Analyse the rhyme scheme in the verse, and the structure of the verse as couplets (two-line bits)
- Find out if any rhymes then come back later in the verse, if so what effect does that have?
- Analyse what is taken forward by each new verse of the song. Is anything revealed that was hidden before?
- Encourage students to base their verses on the same model

FINISHING THE SONG

By now, students should have a song structured Verse 1, Chorus , Verse 2. (There may be more or fewer than two verses.) In a six-week project, students may only get as far as this, and it is a good achievement if they do. But if they have the opportunity, they could now extend and refine what they have already written. The student prompt sheets are designed to provide some questions and ideas students might consider if they are unsure about how to finish their song.

PERFORMING AND RECORDING THE SONG

Performance opportunities can provide motivation for students to finish their songs, and also a sense of achievement when performing music of their own creation to others. Therefore, we would strongly recommend building in some form of performance at the end of any songwriting project – either recording student work and uploading it to NUMU (**www.numu.org.uk**), students performing to their classmates, or performing in a school or local concert.

NOTE
Your Music Service, Local Authority, local radio stations or other organisation may well run songwriting competitions for young emerging talent in which your students could enter their class-work into. Also, NUMU (**www.numu.org.uk**) is a great way for students to publish their own music, as well as receiving reviews and comments from other students.

OPTIONAL OUT-OF-HOURS LINK

Consider establishing a songwriting club, ideally with a music technology link, for budding songwriters to continue with their work. The *Writers Unblocked* resource developed by the Leeds pathfinders, gives some ideas for developing songwriting as an extra-curricular activity. Download it from **www.musicalfutures.org.uk/songwriting**

GENERAL

- Regular and frequent peer review of developing work is important as this helps students to see how others' work is developing
- As an end assessment for the unit, give each student a sheet with basic levelling criteria on and ask them to mark every group's songs. They should be asked to find positive things to say as well as questions they would like to ask the writers about anything they felt didn't work as well

- Ensure that students with Special Educational Needs receive the right sort of support – either focused teacher support or older students working alongside students
- Stretch Gifted and Talented students by asking them to compose in a style which is unfamiliar to them, or setting a challenging topic for the song
- Encourage students to make use of music technology (for example creating beats/backing tracks to rap over) where appropriate
- Upload student's songs to NUMU (**www.numu.org.uk**), and use the blogging tool as a means of recording musical and lyrical ideas as songs progress
- Consider developing a cross-curricular project with the English department, with lyric-writing forming part of a creative writing course

FAQS: SONGWRITING

The following provides some guidance on questions that may come up when running a songwriting project.

Should students use rhymes in their lyrics?

Rhymes play an important role in the effect of a song. Because people expect them, there is often a feeling of disappointment if they are not there. However this doesn't necessarily mean they have to be used.

If students need a rhyme, but can't find one, they could try changing the order of words in the sentence to have a different one at the end (for example 'leave for the town right away' changed to 'leave right away for the town'). However, no rhyme at all is usually better than a sentence which doesn't sound right (for example 'right away, for the town you must leave').

A half-rhyme can sometimes be used. For example, 'town' and 'now' are sort of rhymes in:

'Really got to go,

Got to get to town,

There's no time to lose,

I must be there now'

However, if this gets taken too far it often doesn't work. This will depend on other things, such as how rhymes are used elsewhere in the song. Encourage students to try saying the phrase out loud and listen to it carefully. If they have to do this a few times before they are happy with it, it probably isn't good enough. Rhymes need to be made by matching the strong syllables: 'singing' rhymes with 'ringing' and not with 'one thing'.

GUIDE TO SONGWRITING

Another professional songwriter trick is to use the same word again, for example:

'There's no time to lose,

Got to get to town,

It's all far too late, and I

Have to be in town'

A rhyming dictionary can be a useful resource to have available for students to refer to. Or they could write their own collection, based on the topic of the song.

Does it matter if it is difficult to sing the words?

This doesn't matter provided that somebody <u>can</u> sing the words. But as students probably won't want their songs to be show-off pieces for clever singers, encourage them to do all they can to make the words singable, either by changing the speed or rewriting the music.

Using one note per syllable can work well (unless students are looking for a specific effect). It is always effective to match strong beats, rhymes and words which are important to the message of the song.

Some words are more easily sung on high notes than others and some words are more easily sung in fast succession than others. Changing words can often help, for example 'get down quickly, please take care' is more difficult to sing quickly than 'come on down and take more care'. (Students could be asked to analyse why.)

If the words could easily be mistaken for others, this could either be a disaster or a triumph depending on what effect your students want. (Did he sing 'robber banned' or 'rubber band'?)

Does the rhythm come first from the words or the music?

It depends, and it could be either, but what is important is that the words and music fit well together rhythmically.

When speaking the words, you would be unlikely to have long extended syllables in the way that you do when singing. From this point of view, the music is more important in giving the rhythm. But in all other respects it is the other way around, the song will work if the rhythm fits the words and it won't work if the rhythm doesn't fit the words.

What if a student is struggling with writing tunes to lyrics?

Encourage your students to repeat their lyrics in rhyme with the accompaniment, and gradually a simple tune should come. If it doesn't, they could try writing a simple chord sequence and choosing one or two of the notes of each chord in turn, singing the words on those notes until the chord changes. Then sing the next bit on notes from the next chord. Again, a tune is likely to emerge gradually. Another approach is to write the tune first and then add the lyrics.

Often, during the course of working on a song, the tune will change as people keep singing it, and this can mean it gets better.

GUIDE TO SONGWRITING

One of my students' songs sounds like somebody else's, but they don't want to make big changes.

Sometimes changing just one small part of a tune can make a lot of difference, especially if it is the first, last or highest note. Encourage your students to try to find another note which fits with the chord and carry on from there. Then, they may be happy to move a few more notes around.

Another method is to keep the notes the same but change the rhythm. For example, a tune that starts with four even notes will sound very different if you make the first note longer and the next three shorter. This may also mean changing the words.

Students may also consider changing the chords. This can have a surprisingly strong effect on how the tune sounds.

What if the verse and chorus sounds the same?

Suggest that your students try:

- Changing the harmonies within either the verse or the chorus
- Changing the key within either the verse or the chorus
- Putting the musical lines in a different order
- Adding an extra line in the verse, possibly a repeat
- Changing the texture or the basic beat (for example swing the chorus)

Alternatively, unless their song is of the kind where this doesn't matter (as in some kinds of Blues, for example) it might be worth writing a new tune for one of the sections.

Students are saying their song sounds boring

Is this because they keep repeating the same idea? Could they say the same thing in different ways? Encourage them to try changing one or two words to see what happens. Or try changing where the main word (which relates to the topic of the song) is placed; at the very beginning or end of a line is often good. Changing the order of the verses may help.

In a good song, there should be a balance between repeated elements and new things. This will depend partly on the style of the song. It is worth students analysing good songs to find the moment when something new is brought in.

Sometimes, words sound dull because they are not focused on one subject and wander between different ideas. Unless this is the whole point of the song, students could improve lyrics by making sure that they keep to the subject. You could also encourage them to think of a new image to express their ideas (if something is boring, maybe it feels like having to 'live with your head full of porridge'; if someone is beautiful, maybe that person 'makes you feel like rain is made of fizzy blue water') or to come up with a surprising way of saying what you think, by exaggerating ('the lesson lasted a million years') or using unexpected words ('he plays football like a soapy superstar').

The effect of a song comes from all of its elements, so what may sound a dull lyric when spoken can be fantastic when sung. Other helpful changes may arise from considering the following:

GUIDE TO SONGWRITING

○ Does the music contain too many lines with the same tune following one another?

○ Do the chords always come in the same order and end the same way?

○ Does the bass line only ever play the main chord note on the first beat of the bar?

○ Could the highest note in the tune get moved towards the end of the section?

○ Could the rhythm in the accompaniment get adjusted slightly to change the feel?

○ Is the tempo right?

○ Is the texture always the same?

What if the group disagrees about something in the song?

This can be the result of having a few students with strong creative ideas in the same group. Encourage everyone to try out all of the ideas, ensuring everybody's suggestions get heard. They may then discover what works best, and choose from all the available material.

Encourage students to play different versions of the song to other people – students from other groups for example – whose opinions they trust, and ask for comments.

Sometimes, a compromise is possible (using different versions in different verses, for example). But ultimately students are going to have to go with one agreed song. If they are performing it themselves, encourage them to go for what they can perform best.

PROJECT SNAPSHOT

The following splits the materials into six lessons. The various interlinked activities are separated out as individual exercises, but students should be reminded that, when they write a song on their own, they may want to deal with things in a completely different order. This process could and should take place over as many weeks as students need; some exercises may each need two or three lessons. This is just a guide to illustrate one way of structuring a songwriting module in a six-week period.

Lesson	Content
1	• Introduction to songwriting project *(5 mins)* • Discussion of song topic ideas and lyric ideas *(10 mins)* • Students go into small groups and begin working on song topic and lyric ideas *(40 mins)* • End discussion: initial ideas and problems *(5 mins)*
2	• Introduction and discussion of developing and reviewing lyrics *(10 mins)* • Students in small groups continue working on topic and lyrics *(40 mins)* • End discussion, sharing of some lyrics *(10 mins)*
3	• Introduction and explanation of jamming on musical ideas and improvisation *(10 mins)* • Students in small groups begin creating musical material through jamming and improvising *(40 mins)* • End discussion: problems, ways forward, etc *(10 mins)*
4	• Introduction and discussion of writing a chorus *(10 mins)* • Students in small groups begin to write a chorus for their song *(40 mins)* • End discussion, some performances *(10 mins)*
5	• Introduction and discussion of writing a verse *(10 mins)* • Students in small groups begin to write a verse for their song *(40 mins)* • End discussion, showing session *(10 mins)*
6	• Introduction and discussion of putting verse and chorus together *(10 mins)* • Students in small groups practice putting their verse and chorus together *(20 mins)* • Final performances, recording session, evaluation *(30 mins)*

Image Junction

This project enables students to explore how music compliments the moving image by participating in a multimedia performance event combining music technology and live performance on instruments.

This project is split into three sections:

1. Understanding minimalism through listening, composing and performing, and creating a backing track

2. Composing drum loops (using music technology) and riffs (on acoustic/electronic instruments) using minimalist composing techniques

3. Rehearsing and performing as a whole class to create a complete soundtrack for a short film over a backing track

PREPARATION

○ Research suitable films (see below)

○ Produce a template to highlight key events in the film (with timings) as a tool for structuring the soundtrack and cueing performers

○ Prepare a worksheet based around your minimalist piece that enables students to identify specific composing techniques, or download the sample worksheet provided on **www.musicalfutures.org.uk/image+junction**

○ Organise a final performance, for example a class performance, performance in assembly, in an out-of-school context, etc

SELECTING A FILM

This project requires you to select a short film (no more than four minutes long) to use with your students. Films that are royalty free for educational use can be found on **www.archive.org/details/opensource_movies**. Films will be most suitable if they have little or no dialogue and have a natural rhythm: avoid those that might encourage isolated sound effects.

VIDEO LINK

The film *Boom Bip* used in the Nottingham City pilot for this project is available from **www.musicalfutures.org.uk/image+junction**

RESOURCES

○ Laptop/projector/screen to show the film

○ ICT facilities with computers running sequencing software (for example Acid Xpress (PC), Garageband (Mac users) or suitable alternatives). Audacity editing software may also be useful and is available free from **http://audacity.sourceforge.net/)**

○ Enough instruments for your students to divide into three or four groups (depending on what is available). For example:

→ Bass guitars

→ Lead guitars

→ Violins or other accessible melodic instrument

→ Tuned percussion or keyboards

○ Three or four breakout spaces for the instrumental sessions, as well as a suitable space for the whole class to play their instruments

○ A powerful PA to play the backing track loudly enough for students to perform their live parts on top – if they can't hear their drum loops, it is extremely difficult to play together. (It is also crucial that the backing track features a strong simple drum loop that students can clearly hear and 'lock' to)

○ Recording equipment

○ Music leaders for the instrumental work sessions. (The information on using additional support in the classroom in the Band Instrumental Work project (page 47) also applies here)

Our suggestions here are based on previous Image Junction projects in schools. However, you can adapt this project to the instruments that you have in your department.

EXPLORING MINIMALISM: PERFORMING

WARMING UP: PHASE SHIFTING

Divide the class into two groups, and get them to repeatedly clap this football-chant rhythm:

Ask one group to add an extra beat (a shout, stomp, etc) at the end of each repetition, while the other group continues clapping the 'normal' rhythm, resulting in the two groups going out of phase by one beat, until they eventually come together again.

IMAGE JUNCTION

EXPLORING MINIMALISM: LISTENING AND UNDERSTANDING

The following are examples of minimalist tracks available for download on ITunes, which are suitable for listening exercises:

- *Block Rockin' Beats* or *One Too Many Mornings* – Chemical Brothers (Be careful of language on other tracks on this album)

- *Different Trains* – Steve Reich

- *Elements* – Lemon Jelly

- *Neqoyqatsi* – Philip Glass

A sample worksheet is available on **www.musicalfutures.org.uk/ image+junction** which highlights minimalist techniques (for example repetition, repetition with slight changes, subtractive melodies, layering loops over time, phase shifting, etc).

EXPLORING MINIMALISM: COMPOSING

Using tuned percussion instruments (or keyboards) over a backing beat (for example a drum loop):

- Create a short pattern (based around a G pentatonic scale) that students can 'loop' in time with the backing track. You can use any mode/scale here, however we have made suggestions throughout this project based on G pentatonic

- Practise altering the pattern by adding or subtracting a note

- Practise altering the pattern by changing the pitch of one note

- In pairs, practise repeating the original version and one of the altered versions on top of each other

- Identify one of the patterns produced by the students and ask the composer of the chosen melodic pattern to teach it to the rest of the group

- Record the whole group performing, keeping in time with the backing track

- Listen to the recording and ask students to create a new part that acts as a rhythmic counterpoint

- Practise playing both parts together. Keep this recording as it can link into the live instrumental work later on in the unit

ALTERNATIVE ACTIVITY

- Translate the football chant phase-shifting exercise into a melodic pattern and practise in pairs, with one student holding the original part against a beat, and the other playing the shifting part, then swap

- Use a sequencer to experiment with all of the above techniques

COMPOSING A BACKING TRACK USING MUSIC TECHNOLOGY

Using your chosen music technology software, students create their own film backing track made up of short minimalist loops:

- Find and audition up to ten drum loops from the sample library of your chosen sequencing/looping software or, preferably, explore with students what makes a good drum pattern, and use software to create and audition their own drum patterns using an input grid. Stress the need for a clear beat for live performers to play to

- Show students how to set up a loop lasting no more than eight bars and using chosen sounds/effects

- Play students' loops and ask the class to make decisions about which are the most effective loops and/or structures, and which are likely to be most effective as backing tracks for the film

- Save the work, so that an overall backing track for the film can be put together from students' ideas

- Mix the music technology backings created by the students so that the overall backing track is synched to the film

COMPOSING MINIMALIST LOOPS ON INSTRUMENTS

- Explain to students that they will be creating patterns on instruments in small groups to build up a minimalist piece in layers. Their loops should be grounded in G pentatonic so they can fit together later

- Explain that they will also need to use at least one of the minimalist techniques discussed in earlier sessions

- Split the class into three/four instrumental groups – based on what instruments and space you have in your department

This process could last anything between two to four weeks.

In instrumental groups, music leaders should cover the following:

- Recap on instruments and playing techniques (this is presuming that this unit will follow some sort of skills-based project, for example Band Instrumental Work, page 88)

- Recap the G pentatonic scale and identify relevant notes on the instruments. Core loops should be based around a G pentatonic scale: individual loops may evolve later by introducing different notes (in minimalist style) against the G pentatonic background

- Create minimalist loops using a range of stimuli including the backing track and film action as starting points

- Explore how to use additive/subtractive techniques, layering of loops and phase shifting to develop the loops. Help students to experiment with this, as well as extended instrumental techniques, share their ideas with the group, and come to a group decision about the final version

- Encourage students to evaluate their own loops, identify the most effective ones, and then teach these to the rest of the group

IMAGE JUNCTION

- Encourage students to notate their loops using stave or graphic notation to help them remember for subsequent weeks

- Practise the final version of the instrumental loops keeping in time with the backing track: what features of the backing track do they need to listen out for in order to 'lock' with it?

While students are creating instrumental loops, it is critical that they work with the backing track (as created in the music technology sessions), otherwise they may create loops that don't fit with the groove or sit naturally at the agreed tempo.

SPECIFIC INSTRUMENTAL GUIDANCE

The following is based on instruments that have been used for this project in Musical Futures schools. However this guidance can be adapted for use with any available instruments.

Violin

- Distribute instruments and encourage students to make sounds on them

- Demonstrate how to hold the violin, and introduce pizzicato. Encourage students to practise plucking different strings

- Carry out a call and response exercise on different strings

- Demonstrate bow hold and encourage students to practise bowing different strings

- Get the whole group to play call and response bowed patterns

- Introduce extended techniques such as tremolo, col legno, glissando to advanced students

Please note this is written as if this is students' first experience of playing a violin. If they are already familiar with the instrument, please adapt accordingly.

Bass/guitar

- Introduce sound manipulation (volume swells on bass/guitar, manipulation of equalisation on amps/guitars, etc)

- Practise playing on different strings

- Recap correct left-hand finger technique

- Carry out a call and response exercise using left hand notes

- Introduce extended techniques such as note bending, slaps, etc

Keyboard

- Recap G pentatonic scale and how to build chords from these notes

- Introduce different playing techniques (broken chords, legato/staccato, etc)

- Experiment with different sounds to get the right timbre and quality of attack for each loop

PUTTING IT TOGETHER

When your students are satisfied with their instrumental loops, bring all of the groups back together to fit their parts to the film and the backing track.

Discuss the role of the conductor with students and what various signals mean. Explain any signals that you are going to use beforehand (or consider developing signals in consultation with your students – see also the Guide to Classroom Workshopping (page 47) for some ideas about cues and signals). Demonstrate signals for 'start', 'stop', 'crescendo/decrescendo', etc.

- Set up the layout of the 'orchestra sections'
- Start the backing track and signal instrumental sections to perform their loops in time with the backing track. Use the graphic score you have developed as cues for individual loops
- Play the film and run the recorded backing track while conducting the live instruments over the top
- Discuss factors to consider when students are evaluating their work (for example playing in time, balance, contrast, placement of different loops, structure, dramatic effectiveness)
- Rehearse loops in instrumental groups
- Encourage students to use dynamics and different textures/timbres to refine their performance

PUBLIC SCREENING/PERFORMANCE

Plan with your students whether their performance will happen in lesson time (ideally film the session), or whether there will be a 'public screening' – for example all classes in assembly, for parents/carers in a concert, etc. After the performance, encourage students to write a review of the soundtrack.

OPTIONAL OUT-OF-HOURS LINK

After-school sessions for this project can include the opportunity for students to extend skills on music technology or any of the 'live' instruments. Students can also work with music leaders as a production team, making decisions about how to build the music technology loops into the overall film backing track and how to structure the interim and final film timelines.

IMAGE JUNCTION

PROJECT SNAPSHOT

This project could take between five to eight weeks, therefore the timings will need to shift accordingly

Lesson	Content
1	• Introduce the project • Show students the film • Exploration of minimalist techniques through listening/performing
2	• Introduce students to composing drum loops on sequencing software • Students work on composing their own drum loops • Decide which loops to use for the backing track
3	• Show students the film with the remixed backing track • Students work in small groups creating loops on instruments, practicing loops against backing track • Listen to performances of instrumental loops as a whole class by each of the groups
4	• Decide how to structure the loops in relation to the film for maximum effect • Explain the role of the conductor, signalling etc • Work with the whole class on instruments performing to the backing track and film
5	• Final performance/practice for assembly, concert • Evaluation/feedback

Case Study: Morpeth Secondary School

Morpeth School is a secondary school with nearly 1,200 students situated in Bethnal Green – an ethnically diverse area that has some of the most endemic poverty in the London Borough of Tower Hamlets. Students come from a wide range of ethnic backgrounds with those of Bangladeshi heritage forming just over half of the school's population. A high proportion of the students use English as an additional language, where the majority of students speak Bengali/Sylheti. The school has an Arts Specialism (Art, Drama and Music).

- Typical class size: 30

- % of students involved in instrumental/vocal tuition: over 25%

- % of students taking KS4 music: 20%

- % of students involved in extra-curricular music projects: all students are involved at different stages throughout their schooling, beginning in Year 6

MORPETH AND MUSICAL FUTURES

Morpeth started exploring Musical Futures in 2005. Now all Year 7, 8 and 9 students participate in Musical Futures, with Year 10 students working along the same model of learning for some Key Stage 4 units.

Peter Romhany, Head of Music, explains their approach to Musical Futures.

GETTING STARTED WITH MUSICAL FUTURES

"I read about Musical Futures, and met one of the teachers piloting it who spoke highly about the possibilities. Also, our local Music Service (Tower Hamlets Arts and Music Service), ran an inset attended by one of our department. We were sceptical at first and decided to trial it in Year 8 with a slightly more formal approach and link it to our schools Learning to Learn project scheme. After the success of this, we trialled it in Year 9 and haven't looked back.

CASE STUDY: MORPETH SECONDARY SCHOOL

WHY MUSICAL FUTURES?

One of our whole-school developmental targets has been to look at ways of helping students become independent learners and develop team skills. The initial focus was with Year 8s and, having been a part of this project-style of working, we felt that this needed to continue in Year 9, which is where Musical Futures fits in. In Year 9, we continue to look at learning styles and the 'Five Rs' (Resilience, Responsibility, Reasoning, Resourcefulness and Reflectiveness) alongside Musical Futures.

Raising student aspiration is another key focus in our school and the teacher-facilitated lessons, creative ensemble work (see the Guide to Classroom Workshopping on page 47) carried out in class and by external groups such as the Guildhall School of Music and Drama, Barbican and Guildhall CONNECT have provided opportunities for students to excel.

MORPETH'S MUSICAL FUTURES APPROACH

Four years ago, our school embarked on a programme of study for Year 8 students who were offered the chance to choose two of six 'Learning Projects'. By splitting the year group in two (eight-form entry), students would undertake their project every two weeks for half a year then change to their new project in the second half of the year. This meant class sizes of 20 with projects beginning at 11.15am and finishing at 3.20pm, leading to reduced numbers in a class and larger chunks of time to work with students. The projects ranged from outdoor leadership skills, filmmaking, animation, rocket building and print design to 'Rock Factory'. At the heart of each project was 'Learning to Learn' – a discovery about learning involving a set of principles, which help learners to learn more effectively and to transfer and utilise these principles across the curriculum.

'Rock Factory' begins with a series of workshops where all students experience drums, guitar, keyboard, singing and bass guitar using a carousel system (In a similar format to the Band Instrumental Skills project, see page XX). At the end of the workshops, students select their favourite instrument and are asked to form bands (often with the help of tutors). All bands then work on the first piece *Wild Thing*, building up the skills required to play their instrument. Next, they choose a song from a selection of 12 pieces including *Black and Gold* (Sam Sparro), *Song 2* (Blur), *Fly Away* (Lenny Kravitz), *Seven Nation Army* (White Stripes), *Knocking on Heavens Door* (Bob Dylan), *Word Up* (Cameo) and *Hell Ain't A Bad Place to Be* (ACDC).

It is important to ensure milestones are set along the way, so we include informal showing sessions, a semi-formal performance of *Wild Thing*, and then a 'Battle of The Bands', where all eight bands compete against each other for the top prize of a recording contract (showcased on our record label on NUMU) and a performance in the Year 8 Project Showcase. At the end of the year, 80 students had formed 16 rock bands and developed strong instrumental and team skills. Alongside this, they discovered more about learning styles including the 'Five Rs'. Another interesting aspect of this project was that students were not assessed using traditional methods, instead they responded to their own views and those of others, working towards a real-life outcome, which they could relate to. This

NOTE

See the Musical Futures website **www.musicalfutures.org.uk/assessment** for the assessment framework Morpeth uses.

CASE STUDY: MORPETH SECONDARY SCHOOL

included learning charts where students map their progress relating to the 'Five Rs'. All students keep learning-journals and use these in each session to write about the work they carried out during the day and comment on the focus of the day. The performances and milestone tasks help us to monitor learners' progress throughout the sessions with the final performance as a measure of their success.

We introduced the informal learning model of Musical Futures in Year 9 with a number of classes as a trial to see how we could best manage it. We offered this alongside our regular curriculum to measure progress and responses from students. We were in the fortunate position of being able to run two Year 9 classes (60 students) at once having three teachers timetabled, reducing class sizes to 20. We decided that one teacher would offer an ICT songwriting project in our new Mac Suite, while the other two taught either Musical Futures or our regular curriculum. The classes worked on a rotation system with ten students from each class per term working on the ICT project. When they completed the piece, it was uploaded to their NUMU webpage and in some cases blue-toothed to their phones. Students responded extremely well to this and produced high-quality compositions. Having a 'real-life' outcome the students could relate to encouraged them to complete work to a higher level.

It became apparent that the students working along the Musical Futures path (instead of our regular curriculum offer at the time) were more engaged, there were less behavioural issues, students were completing work to a higher standard and we were able to continue our 'Learning to Learn' work more effectively, developing the 'Five Rs' further. The students who had taken part in 'Rock Factory' in Year 8 were also able to continue playing their instruments and lead groups, generating a positive atmosphere. These students had experienced a high standard of performance in 'Rock Factory' and strived for this again in Year 9, motivating others.

Another feature of our work is the teacher facilitated, creative ensemble work, which began ten years ago with the Guildhall School of Music and Drama. This was a transition project we set up around our feeder primary schools and instrumental players at the time. The style of working also proved a valuable learning experience for our staff and from this we began delivering creative ensemble lessons in class.

We usually decide on a theme and then let the students create the piece by adding motifs, riffs, etc along the way. The unit would initially begin with warm-up games getting students comfortable with pulse, movement and each other then choosing a few students who demonstrated strong rhythmic skills to form the rhythm section. From here, the piece builds up with various themes and changing textures. All students take part and form the creative ensemble. We also do this with whole class 'Cover Songs' where we form a rhythm section and have others playing and singing various parts on top. (See the Guide to Classroom Workshopping, page 47 for a demonstration of this way of working.)

We are now able to teach classes in larger chunks of time, so rather than one lesson a week for Key Stage 3, we have introduced double lessons every two weeks for Year 9 but with smaller class sizes, and are looking at developing day/week long projects across KS3, using our community links to facilitate this.

CASE STUDY: MORPETH SECONDARY SCHOOL

RESOURCING MUSICAL FUTURES

By taking part in the initial school Year 8 Learning to Learn scheme, we were able to secure funding for a range of instruments to run four rock bands. As this success continued and we needed more instruments to run Year 9 Musical Futures, we used the Specialism budget. When I set up the initial Instrumental Scheme 15 years ago, the school had a link with a Bankers Trust at the time and I approached them for funding for instruments. Our links with external organisations such as Barbican Education have also provided us with resources in terms of equipment and personnel.

We have recently looked at ways of minimising disruption for other departments around us in terms of soundproofing and have chosen instruments and amps which require little space, less volume and have multiple inputs. This has enabled us to set up group work in small and often unusual places.

TEACHING STYLES

At first, we found the hardest part of delivering Musical Futures the belief that students would respond appropriately, and to 'let go' of the usual management of students in a classroom. Our time now is spent problem solving with students, acting as mentors and looking at learning styles. We feel that our students are now experiencing a more real approach to music making and as such respond better given the choices and responsibility. We continue to look at ways of developing our delivery of Musical Futures and to build resources that make it easier to manage.

IMPACT ON STUDENTS

At the end of the first year with Year 8 'Rock Factory', feedback from students was very positive. Attendance across the year group on the project day was greater than normal and student uptake with instrumental tuition rose – particularly those of Bangladeshi origin who wanted to learn electric guitar, singing, drumming, and bass guitar. Even more noticeable was the number of girls who wanted to play and form their own bands. When asked how 'Rock Factory' differed from the usual experience of school, student responses included 'It's more enjoyable', 'There's less written work and it's more hands on', 'You learn more about yourself', 'It's not boring and I want to do it' and 'Rock Factory is more interactive'.

Now in our third year of the full programme with Key Stage 3, other positive outcomes include the uptake of music in Year 10, the number of students wanting to learn instruments and join existing school performance groups, students independently forming their own bands and a more balanced gender and ethnic involvement in extra-curricular music.

CASE STUDY: MORPETH SECONDARY SCHOOL

EXTRA-CURRICULAR WORK

We have needed to add extra hours to peripatetic teaching to accommodate all of the students who wish to learn an instrument and we've added additional lessons such as Rock Band Tuition. The use of the department at lunchtime has increased as students take on responsibility for developing their own groups and organising rehearsals. We are in the process of working with external agencies and venues to provide an outlet for more regular gigs that we hope will eventually be managed and run by Diploma students.

ADVICE FOR OTHERS CONSIDERING MUSICAL FUTURES?

Think of your overall plan and where you would like your department to be in the future. Keep it manageable to begin with and, over time, you will see the benefits. We filmed the work early on as evidence to take back to whole school staff and senior management, in order to gain support and they then became active members of learning working parties. Informing staff about what you are doing and showing evidence can lead to support from the rest of the school. Look at external links and how you can utilise these in your school, providing opportunities for students which raise aspirations. **"**

Morpeth School is a Musical Futures Champion School

Informal Learning

Introduction

The informal learning in the music classroom model aims to enhance student motivation, enjoyment and skill-acquisition in music lessons by tapping into the real-life learning practices of popular musicians. It is designed particularly with the Year 9 age group in mind, however the informal learning model has successfully been adapted for Year 8, and even Year 7 and Year 10/11 students.

Most music teachers would place the motivation of their students high on their list of priorities, not only because motivation is an end in itself, but also because it is a prime building-block in the acquisition of musical skills and knowledge. While motivating students during lessons is therefore a priority, teachers also want to make their lessons connect with the huge enjoyment that students get from music in their lives beyond the school.

Numerous attempts have been made to close the gap between students' own musical culture and that of the classroom. As teachers are well aware, popular music was first brought into schooling over three decades ago in attempts to connect with students' interests. However, while popular music today does form a major part of curriculum content, the informal learning practices of the musicians who create it have not generally been recognised or adopted as teaching and learning strategies within classrooms. Popular music itself may have been present in most classrooms, but the ways in which it is created and passed on in the world outside school have been missing.

THE FIVE PRINCIPLES OF INFORMAL LEARNING

At the heart of popular music's transmission processes lie informal learning practices, through which all popular musicians pass in one way or another.

The informal learning model is therefore based around **five key principles**:

1. **Learning music that students choose, like and identify with**, as opposed to being introduced to music which is often new and unfamiliar, and chosen by a teacher

2. **Learning by listening and copying recordings**, as opposed to learning through notation or other written/verbal instructions

3. **Learning alongside friends**, instead of learning through instruction with continuous adult guidance

4. **Assimilating skills and knowledge in personal ways** according to musical preferences, starting with whole 'real world' pieces of music, as opposed to following a designated progression from simple to complex, involving specially-composed music, a curriculum or a graded syllabus

5. **Maintaining a close integration of listening, performing, improvising and composing** throughout the learning process, as opposed to gradually specialising and differentiating between listening, performing, improvising and composing skills

All aspects of the classroom practice of informal learning draw on, and attempt to replicate as closely as possible, two or more of these five key principles.

FURTHER READING

Please see the first edition **www. musicalfutures.org.uk/c/first+edition** for a detailed set of responses from students and teachers in the pilot phase. See also Professor Lucy Green's *Music, Informal Learning and the School* (Ashgate, 2008) for an in-depth analysis of the learning processes of students and the experiences of teachers in the informal learning model.

BENEFITS

When schools implement the informal learning model successfully, they tend to see a combination of the following occur.

Motivation among students increases, often quite dramatically. This can be reflected by students staying on task in lessons for the majority of the time, by improved behaviour, and by students noticeably enjoying their music lessons. Also student attitude tends to improve – towards music lessons and the music department – with students sometimes extending their work beyond lessons and staying behind in lunchtimes, breaks and after school. This also can manifest by teachers hearing of students enthusiastically discussing their work in music outside of the music department, which in turn can help to raise the profile of the music department within the school.

The informal learning model often facilitates the development of instrumental and vocal skills among students, particularly listening skills as integrated listening is at the heart of this approach. Teachers/practitioners often find that students have musical skills that they were unaware of, and are able to show these skills in music lessons in a way that they hadn't been able to, or felt confident to, previously.

Apart from musical skills, students tend to develop a range of non-

INTRODUCTION

musical skills – such as leadership skills, teamwork skills, learning how to listen and cooperate with others, and negotiation skills. Students often emerge as being natural leaders, and these are not always the students their teachers would expect to take on such roles.

Schools often witness a significant improvement in the take-up of music at Key Stage 4, in some cases with classes doubling or even tripling. Students tend to be keen to continue with music outside of music lessons, either by taking-up instrumental and/or vocal tuition, to become involved in extra-curricular activities, or both.

Teachers often state that running the informal learning model with their Key Stage 3 students can lead them to change aspects of their practice to incorporate informal learning across their teaching, from Year 7 to Year 13.

FURTHER READING

Music, Informal Learning and the School: A New Classroom Pedagogy (Lucy Green, Ashgate Publishers, 2008)	An in-depth critical exploration by the informal learning model research director, of how the model impacted on students and teachers
How Popular Musicians Learn: A Way Ahead for Music Education (Lucy Green, Ashgate Publishers, 2002)	The ideas behind the informal learning model derive from research undertaken for this book, where one of the outcomes was a number of suggestions for incorporating informal learning into classroom and instrumental teaching strategies

Implementing Informal Learning

This section provides start-up advice and frequently asked questions to guide teachers/practitioners through the process of delivering the informal learning model. While the five principles at the heart of the informal learning model (see page 131) form the core of the approach, the programme of activities, and the way it can be integrated into a music department is flexible.

ROLE OF THE TEACHER

The role of the teacher (or other practitioner) is perhaps the most interesting as well as the most challenging aspect of the informal learning model.

The exact role of the teacher is difficult to put into words, and it varies depending on the context and on the personalities of the individuals involved.

In the first lesson of each project, students are given a task by their teacher. Throughout each project, resources are organised by the teacher; ground rules, such as respect for instruments, staff and other students, are laid down and maintained by the teacher; and in all similar respects the teacher's role is no different from what would normally be expected in the classroom. But following this, teachers should enter into a process of standing back, observing students, and offering help, guidance and support (usually via musical modelling) based very much on what the students have decided they want to achieve.

In brief the role of the teacher/practitioner is as follows:

Set the task going
Stand back
Observe
Diagnose
Guide
Suggest
Model
Take on students' perspectives
Help students achieve the objectives they set for themselves

IMPLEMENTING INFORMAL LEARNING

While the roles of teachers and students can feel different from a 'normal' classroom situation, it is essential that ground rules about acceptable behaviour are laid down clearly from the outset. Different teachers will have their own ground rules and ways of communicating these to students, and they include such things as staying in designated rooms, treating other people with respect, treating equipment with respect, etc. Classroom rules still apply, and there will of course be situations where teachers have to discipline students and even remove them from the classroom if they are being disruptive.

Where the informal learning model is most successful, the music teacher already has a good rapport with students, and can firmly establish ground rules without needing to overstate them. Newly-qualified teachers and student teachers have tried and succeeded with this model, however we strongly recommend that where possible a Head of Music is fully supportive of them, otherwise it can be an unrewarding experience for the teacher and students.

Many teachers experience a number of doubts during the first few lessons, including at times feelings of despair and concern about how students could possibly achieve any worthwhile outcomes. However, when this happens, if teachers give the students a little more time, in most situations students themselves decide that they want to progress. This can have a far greater impact than if the teacher had either stopped the project or had intervened and instructed students to work. In the informal realm it is quite normal for learners to get worse before they get better. You may feel slightly redundant at times, and as if you're not 'teaching' the students anything. However once students start working on instruments, they begin to need more help and this can all change quite quickly. You will inevitably then find yourself highly in demand, and able to share your skills, knowledge and experience with students.

It is also common for teachers to learn alongside their students, especially when working on music with which teachers are not necessarily familiar. This willingness to adapt as a learner alongside your students, and to react to the challenges informal learning poses, is often key to developing a good relationship and a sense of trust and respect between yourself and your students.

The role that the teacher/practitioner takes on within the informal learning model can be critical to its success. The following illustrates some typical situations found in the informal learning model, and how to deal with them in practice:

NOTE

The case study of Oasis Academy Lord's Hill on page 164 contains some insightful reflection on the teacher's role in the informal learning model.

Situation	Don't	Do
A group of students has chosen to copy a song which you think is too hard for them.	Tell them they shouldn't do the difficult song and insist they choose another one.	Say nothing about their choice of song. It is very important that students are free to make their own choices. By trying the copying task they will gradually learn to make more suitable choices for themselves.
A student is attempting to play a difficult melody on the keyboard.	Tell the student that what they are attempting is too difficult for them, devise a simpler part for them to play, and stand over them to ensure they get it right.	Model the melody part yourself, using a simplified version if it seems appropriate, showing the student where the notes are; then leave the student on their own to continue working on their part. They are then able to accept or reject your advice based on their own decisions.
A student who has never played the bass guitar before is holding the instrument flat on their lap, making it difficult to depress the strings.	Tell the student they are holding the instrument incorrectly, show them how to hold it correctly, and insist that they maintain that hold.	Nothing at first. Allow the student to experiment in their own way with holding the instrument. After some time, perhaps even a few lessons later, when you feel the student is receptive, suggest they might find it easier if they hold the instrument differently. Show them how, and then leave the room.
Four students with behavioural problems have grouped themselves together as a friendship group.	Insist that they are not allowed to work together and move them into other groups.	Give them some time to work alone, showing that you trust them to work independently. If they are struggling to organise themselves, start to model rhythms, harmonies, melodies etc for them – hopefully engaging one student who will later start to organise their peers.
Students are unable to decide what instruments to play, as they maintain that none of them are good at music.	Assign instruments to them and give them basic notes to play on these instruments.	Start by discussing with the students their own musical interests, whether any of them sing in an informal way outside of school. Encourage them to try different instruments, and reassure them that this is about the learning process, not necessarily about how good they are at the end of it. Model some notes from the students' chosen song on different instruments, then leave the students to experiment themselves before offering further guidance.
Students are playing their parts and are not listening to each other, and have been doing this most of the time for two lessons.	Tell the students to put down their instruments and listen to you, and organise the students yourself. Stay in the room to make sure they have listened to your advice.	Spend a few minutes in the room listening to the students' work and observing their behaviour, and then approach one member of the group (for example the drummer) and suggest that they take the lead in the group and organise their peers. Encourage them to discuss what is important when in a band (i.e. communication and listening to one another), and make a few suggestions as to how they could rehearse their piece together. Then leave the room and allow the students time to absorb your suggestions.

Overall it is essential that the teacher/practitioner works to establish an environment in which students are free to approach the task, and to organise themselves within their groups, in whatever ways they wish – setting their own objectives and steering their own course through learning.

IMPLEMENTING INFORMAL LEARNING

PROGRAMME STRUCTURE

The informal learning model is not a scheme of work, rather an approach to teaching and learning that draws on the real-life practices of musicians in the informal sphere. However, to make this work in the context of a music department we have organised the model into a number of stages or projects, that can be followed through the course of an academic year. Each begins with an existing piece of music, and the students' learning is structured around this. The first sections contain the main ingredients and core activities of the approach, therefore they must come first if the informal learning model is to be put into action. Following this, you can choose to continue with the ideas, can build in other projects which complement informal learning or can develop your own resources. Example 2 in the Embedding Musical Futures section (see page 36) is an illustration of how the informal learning model integrates with other Key Stage 3 provision in one school.

NOTE

The 'Resource Bank' on the Musical Futures website (**www.musicalfutures. org.uk/c/teacher+created**) and the Teaching Music website (**www.teachingmusic.org.uk**) contain examples of resources around informal learning that teachers have developed themselves.

RESOURCES

Enabling your students to work informally can involve some re-organisation of your music department, both in terms of space and equipment. This shouldn't be a deterrent from carrying out the informal learning model – many teachers find ways of making this work within the space and resources they have available (see the Buildings and Space section (page 194) for some guidance on coping with limited space). Or they work hard to make space and equipment available through negotiation with other teachers and senior management.

For this model to work successfully we advise that a music department needs to establish:

- Enough practice spaces for classes to work in groups of three to six students. For most schools this means that the main classroom, plus up to five other nearby spaces are needed. In many cases this has involved corridors, canteens, other classrooms, etc

- A selection of instruments. Ideally this should involve a combination of electronic instruments (guitars, bass guitars, microphones, drum pads, keyboards, etc) with acoustic instruments (especially percussion), and instruments typically found in the classroom

- CD or MP3 players with speakers, one per small group

- Ideally, additional support in the classroom (see below)

- Ideally, access to the Internet for students to download lyrics, tab charts, chord sheets, and to ICT for students wanting to create music electronically

The informal learning model was designed to make use of conventional acoustic and electronic musical instruments. However, there are many ways in which similar principles can be adapted for use with computers and digital music-making, especially for students interested in urban music. Our Equipment and Music Technology section provides some tips for using music technology (see page 185).

ADDITIONAL SUPPORT IN THE CLASSROOM

In many schools the informal learning model is run by the classroom music teacher, often with little or no help. However, where extra support can be offered (even if not on a weekly basis) this can enhance the experience for students, and can complement and support the knowledge, skills and experiences of the classroom teacher.

It is essential that any people offering additional support are fully inducted into the aims and rationale of the approach. Such people may be:

- Another teacher within the school – not necessarily a music teacher but for example someone who has some interest or experience of being a musician

- A peripatetic instrumental teacher

- Community musician

- Parent

- Teaching assistant

- Musically skilled older student from within the school (this can be particularly effectively as they provide peer rather than adult support)

STRUCTURE AND LENGTH OF LESSONS

Teachers/practitioners fit the informal learning model into their normal music lessons, therefore the length of each session will be determined by how long a school music lesson is, and how often the lesson takes place.

If your lessons take place on a fortnightly, or rotation basis we recommend that you have some measure in place to remind students of what they achieved in the previous lesson – for example a student logbook, a video or audio recording of their work uploaded to NUMU **(www.numu.org.uk)**, etc.

Each project gives some guidance for preparing for and implementing the first lesson. We then suggest a six-week structure, which is to be treated as guidance only and should be personalised around your students. The structure within each lesson should be relatively free, with some lessons seeing students spending the entire time working in small groups.

If required, lessons can be structured to demonstrate a starter, main activity and plenary session, and this can be reflected in lesson plans. While students set their own objectives, the teacher/practitioner can establish an overall objective for the project, or for each individual lesson.

IMPLEMENTING INFORMAL LEARNING

ASSESSMENT

The general advice on assessment (page 20) applies here. Many teachers choose to use their own systems of assessment, or use existing assessment criteria. Students choose for themselves, and organise for each other within their groups, tasks that suit different individuals' abilities. Each project contains progression within itself, and naturally builds on students' existing skills. The nature of the progression is implicit, but observable, based on growth in your students' experiences of themselves as musicians.

GROUPING STUDENTS

It is important that students are allowed to work with their friends. This is to replicate the informal learning environment, where young people enjoy, collaborate and experiment with music alongside people with whom they feel comfortable and familiar. Therefore at the start of the informal learning model explain to your students that this will be the case, and that they will be able to choose their working groups. Size of groups inevitably depends upon the number of spaces available, and therefore sometimes the teacher/practitioner will have to determine this.

STUDENT EVALUATION AND FEEDBACK

We recommend that some form of evaluation is carried out on a regular basis. Student feedback can enable you to find out more than usual about what motivates students, what they consider they have learnt, what they found valuable, easy or difficult, and whether they did or did not enjoy the tasks. The evaluation on page 212 is one example of how you might gain feedback from students.

PERFORMANCES

It can be particularly effective to schedule some form of class performance and discussion at frequent intervals during the informal learning model. This might just be work in progress – with students demonstrating a riff, rhythm or vocal line that they have learnt – other times longer and more complete performances can take place.

If a work-in-progress performance is to take place at the end of a lesson, rather than getting the whole class into the main room for group performances, we suggest that the 'audience' walks around the practice spaces to listen to others. This saves time, and avoids moving equipment, and unplugging and re-setting any electrical items. It also means students can perform in the space they are used to rehearsing in, which can result in a better performance.

Performance opportunities such as these can be essential, since peer-assessment, listening to and watching each other are central parts of informal learning practices. Performances can also lead to some successful exchange of knowledge between students; can encourage students to think about presenting themselves to others; and can also engender a sense of healthy competition between the groups!

However not all students will feel comfortable with performing, so you might consider filming or recording groups, and then play back the video/audio recording to the rest of the class. Where possible, students should have the opportunity to perform in broader contexts – for example in school assemblies, concerts, and sometimes in local gigs and concerts taking place in the community.

IMPLEMENTING INFORMAL LEARNING

Frequently Asked Questions

ON THE TEACHER'S ROLE

I feel uncomfortable about leaving students unsupervised, what should I do?

The informal learning model is not about 'unsupervised' learning – you should have a strong presence in the groups on a regular basis. A good teacher in this situation will regularly go into the spaces in which the students are working for short periods of time meaning that the students are aware of the teacher's presence, yet they still feel able to work independently and be trusted. It can help to have an extra pair of hands in this situation, but many teachers do this approach successfully on their own.

At what point should I intervene and help the students?

Unfortunately there is no straightforward answer to this! The point at which intervention happens (i.e. whether this is five minutes into the first lesson or halfway through the third lesson) will depend entirely on your students' needs. It has to depend on your judgment as a teacher. Sometimes teachers can 'stand back' for too long, where some students could have used help and support earlier, whereas sometimes teachers can intervene too early, taking some of the ownership of the learning away from their students.

The key is to consult with the students about what help they need and when they need it, and to offer/model help/guidance in such a way that when you leave the room you have enabled the students to take on board what you have just modelled for them, at their own level. Avoid a situation where you stand over the student until they 'get it right'.

As a teacher I like to be in control all the time – how will I cope with this?

It can be difficult for teachers to stand back and let the students take control of their learning. However, you are not 'out of control' or redundant in any way in the informal learning model. You are critical in establishing the right environment for this to succeed – for example one where students can work independently but within a classroom situation that does still retain control. Some teachers find that spending time standing back and observing students, especially if this is something that they don't normally do, can be quite liberating and has enabled them to learn something new about their students.

ON STUDENTS

What if students group themselves into a large group?

Students sometimes want to work in a group of eight or nine. If possible, allow students to do this as large groups can sometimes be productive. However, it is likely that students will soon realise that working in a group of that size can become unmanageable, and they will decide to split up into two smaller groups themselves. Also, you may find that in larger groups it is more likely that there will be a student who doesn't have a part, or an instrument, and finds it difficult to establish their role in the group (especially if other, more confident students dominate in a group situation). If this happens, consider offering help and support for what that student could do, or encourage them to double drum parts, keyboard parts, etc.

What if a student refuses to play an instrument or sing?

Some individual students tend to spend time sitting and watching, especially during the first few lessons. Learning by listening and watching peers is an important informal learning practice and forms part of one of the five key principles on which the informal learning model is based. Usually in this situation, after a few lessons of assessing what their role is, students will start to pick up an instrument, vocal part, etc, or one of their peers will encourage them to do so. Alternatively, some students take on a 'non-performing' role – for example the task of organising and leading the group, balancing sound levels, offering advice for refining performances to the rest of their group, etc – which are all perfectly valid and acceptable skills and tasks.

I have a student who doesn't have a friendship group, what should I do?

Although this is fairly rare, some students find it difficult to integrate into a friendship group, or are not initially accepted into a group by their peers. Consider dealing with this in a number of ways:

- See if the student is happy to initially work on their own on their favourite song, and allow them to work individually

- After a number of lessons, ask a member of one of the groups if they would consider accepting the student into their group, and giving them a part to play. Ask the student to try to make it work, and to integrate the student into their group, but assure them that if it doesn't work you will work with them to find an alternative

- Ask the student if they would assist you with recording work in progress. Show them how to use audio recording equipment and set them the task of recording their peers' work

- Alternatively, ask the student to prepare reviews of what other students are doing, and to blog about this on NUMU (**www.numu.org.uk**)

What about students with poor behaviour?

It is essential that you establish clear ground rules concerning behaviour at the beginning of the process, to ensure that an atmosphere of trust is established. If students break these rules and persistently misbehave then you must intervene and consider not

IMPLEMENTING INFORMAL LEARNING

allowing them to do practical work. Usually the threat of stopping practical work is enough to encourage them to improve their behaviour. There have been a few instances where teachers have had to stop students from working on the practical activity due to inappropriate behaviour, but this is a tiny minority compared to what teachers would normally expect. Few detentions are handed out, and few students have to be disciplined.

How does this meet the needs of gifted and talented students?

In this way of learning students set their own challenges and objectives, therefore gifted and talented students challenge themselves accordingly. They certainly don't feel that this way of working is in anyway inferior to what they would have experienced in 'normal' music lessons. Additionally this is a different way of working for many students – working independently and by ear – which in itself can be a new challenge. Consider using students who are particularly talented to help coach others, enabling these students to develop leadership and peer coaching skills. See the section on Gifted and Talented students on page 24, for strategies for challenging these students.

How does this meet the Special Educational Needs of some students?

Students with poor behaviour, lower ability or special educational needs aren't necessarily weak musically, and in these environments those students can often excel where they aren't always able to in the rest of the school, or where they may not have excelled in previous music lessons. However for some students the focus on informal, independent learning can prove to be a challenge, and based on this you need to assess additional levels of support these students may require, and whether you need to adapt the approach in any way.

FURTHER READING

Musical Futures and Special Educational Needs is available for download from **www.musicalfutures.org.uk/c/ reports+and+articles** and provides some advice and guidance based on work carried out during the pilot years in three SEN schools. Also see the section on Special Educational Needs students on page 25.

STRUCTURE

Wouldn't it be better to start with Modelling Aural Learning, which seems more structured?

In some cases, Modelling Aural Learning (page 149) appeals more to teachers as a starting point, as it provides more structured guidance. However, part of the reasoning behind In at the Deep End (page 144) is that it encourages students to experiment, and to explore music and learning in their own way. While Modelling Aural Learning follows the principles of informal learning by aural copying and group work, it provides much more structured guidance, and if this is the first approach to the informal learning model for students, it may seem much more like a 'normal lesson', and contain less appeal. In at the Deep End is designed to motivate, inspire and enthuse students about music learning, but also to enable them to discover for themselves what they need to do in order to progress in their music learning. Modelling Aural Learning then provides a much more structured approach to help develop specific musical skills. Also, having done In at the Deep End first, students have a better understanding of what skills they are developing in Modelling Aural Learning, and their motivation therefore tends to remain high.

What about learning musical terminology?

Terminology is introduced throughout the informal learning model, but it is integrated with the practical activity. For example students won't spend a lesson learning about the term 'ostinato', rather they will be learning ostinatos/riffs in their music making, and teachers are then able to articulate this to them during the course of their lessons.

What about notation?

Notation is used in different forms throughout the informal learning model. However it is rarely a starting point – the music comes first, and notation is usually introduced as a means of helping students remember and record what they have done. Students may also wish to download notation, guitar tab, chord sheets etc from the Internet, which is completely within the spirit of this approach.

Should I give instruments to students or allow them to choose?

This depends on how your department is set up, what equipment you have, and how confident you feel with trusting your students with the instruments you have available. You may wish to consider some of the following, all of which are different approaches used by Musical Futures teachers:

- Before students start their practical work, ask them to write a 'wishlist' of instruments their group requires. You then arrange for each group to have as many of the instruments from their wishlist as possible (based on what you have available)

- Stand in the room/cupboard where your instruments are stored and hand out instruments to students, with relevant leads, amps etc as appropriate. This can take up lesson time, but it ensures you are in control of what equipment is going where. Consider giving a trusted 6th former or older student the task of distributing equipment in this way

- Set up the equipment in the practice spaces before each lesson, enabling students to get on with their practical work straightaway. This can be a lot of effort for you. However if you happen to have a set of Key Stage 3 music lessons grouped together on one day it can be an effective way of managing resources

- Have sets of equipment permanently set up in all of your practice rooms (often bolted down/attached to walls as appropriate). This can require careful management, especially if the rooms are also being used for instrumental teaching but can save valuable set-up/set-down time

- Enable your students to freely choose instruments and set them up themselves. Even though this can take some time at the beginning while students get used to what they need to do to set up their 'band', it enables them to learn about taking responsibility for their instruments, and can help to engender an environment of trust and respect

In at the Deep End

In this initial project students are 'dropped into the deep end' with informal learning, emulating as closely as possible the real-life learning practices of young, beginner popular musicians. The guidance below outlines in detail the first lesson, and then makes suggestions for how to implement the project overall. We do not suggest targets and objectives for every lesson, rather the generic aim of listening to a song and copying it is an ongoing objective for students that stretches over a number of lessons. Within this, students set their own goals and objectives.

INFORMAL LEARNING PRINCIPLES

The key principles of informal learning for In at the Deep End are:

- ○ Learning music that students choose, like and identify with
- ○ Learning by listening and copying recordings
- ○ Learning with friends
- ○ Personal, self-directed learning

The fifth principle – the integration of listening, performing, composing and improvising – is not emphasised in this project. However, any students who spontaneously compose and/or improvise as part of their copying activities should of course be encouraged to do so.

PREPARATION

- ○ Ask students in advance to bring their own CDs/MP3s/iPods with speakers to the lesson
- ○ Ensure you have all of the spaces available that you need
- ○ Ensure you have all of the instruments available that you need

RESOURCES

- ○ Students own CDs/MP3s/iPods and speakers
- ○ CD or MP3 players, one per group
- ○ Practice spaces, one per group

SECTION 3: INFORMAL LEARNING

TECHNOLOGY TIP

Online audio streaming sites, for example Spotify, Last.fm, We7 and Deezer, can enable students to save favourite tunes in playlists, and easily access tracks they might not own.

○ Range of instruments – ideally of a typical 'band' set up (drums, guitar, bass, keyboards, microphones), and/or acoustic instruments, classroom percussion, and ideally access to ICT for students wanting to create music electronically

○ Some current chart tracks (to be used in case students forget to bring their own)

DISCUSSION AND EXPLANATION

Begin the project with a brief class discussion of the question: How do you think popular musicians learn to play their instruments; how do they learn to sing, improvise and compose music?

While students may suggest all sorts of ideas, many of which will be correct, generally few students seem to be aware of, or can describe, informal learning approaches. This may differ if the students have already been introduced to similar approaches, or other Musical Futures projects earlier on in Key Stage 3.

Either way, you should ensure that the points below are covered, and profiled, by the end of the discussion:

○ Popular musicians may learn by taking lessons, practising, using computers, and in other ways that students might have suggested

○ But the main thing they all do is learn by listening to music they like, and by copying it

○ They do this by themselves and with friends, rather than through a teacher

○ They make up their own versions of the music – alone and in groups

○ They improvise and compose their own music

Students may suggest that musicians use computers, or engage music producers to make their music for them. These are valid answers, but students should be alerted to the fact that those musicians also spend time listening to and familiarising themselves with other artists' work as part of their own creative processes.

NOTE

Radio 1's 'Live Lounge' involves established artists performing covers of other artists' work. Playing or showing students examples of this can form the basis for useful discussion topics throughout this project, for example about how the musicians 'make the music their own', and how students can relate this to their own music making. See **www.bbc.co.uk/radio1/livelounge/** or search for 'Radio 1 Live Lounge' on **www.youtube.com**

Explain that for the next few lessons students are going to learn informally, as far as possible, by:

○ Working in friendship groups

○ Choosing any song from among their own musical interests (barring unsuitable lyrics)

○ Choosing instruments (or technology)

○ Listening to and copying the song they choose in whatever ways they wish

IN AT THE DEEP END

It should also be explained that:

- Teachers will at first stand back, observe and diagnose, then guide, suggest and model

- Teachers will try to take on students' perspectives, and help students to achieve the objectives that they set for themselves

At this point it is important to establish ground rules concerning the norms of behaviour expected by yourself, the department and the school.

GETTING STARTED

- Ask students to organise themselves into friendship groups. The number of groups may be dictated by the number of spaces you have available

- Students are then instructed to take their CDs/MP3s/iPods and a CD/MP3/iPod player into a practice space and choose one song. (Choosing the song may take the whole of the rest of the lesson, plus some or all of the next lesson)

- If students choose a song immediately, they can then select instruments to play and begin the task

You may feel slightly redundant during this phase, as you may find you have no role to play in helping the students select their songs. Furthermore, the students will be more interested in selecting songs that they like, rather than ones that they think will be easy or suitable to copy. However, it is essential that they are allowed to choose, and that they like and identify with the music they are working on. Therefore no advice should be offered at this point, unless it is explicitly requested by students. If students choose a song which you feel is unsuitable, they will learn that for themselves through the process of attempting to copy it – finding out in this way is likely to be more meaningful.

Once students have chosen their song, it is advisable to make a copy of the song during or after the lesson for safe-keeping. We have often experienced situations where groups expressed frustration and maintained they were unable to work as they did not have the music that they wanted to copy with them.

SONG CHOICE

The only type of song which would be unacceptable for students to work on is a song with sexual, racist or violent lyrics. Most students understand this without the need for it to be underlined, but it may be worth stating at the outset.

It can sometimes take groups of students some time to decide upon a song. Part of the decision-making process often involves discussion

TECHNOLOGY TIP

Music programmes can be used as instruments in themselves, whether this is as a keyboard-triggered 'virtual' instrument, or by creating atmospheric textural 'pads' as a musical backdrop to performances. This can work particularly well when working in various contemporary dance music styles. Where groups are lacking a drummer, it can be helpful to use computer-based music sequencing software to create rhythm tracks, again this can be very effective in dance music styles where a traditional natural drum kit sound may not create the desired rhythmic timbres.

of the music, negotiating, deciding upon pros and cons, etc, so where possible it is best to let this happen without teacher intervention. However, if a decision has not been reached by the middle of the second lesson, you need to find a way of encouraging the group to come to – and stick to – a decision, otherwise they will be given a piece of music to work on from your collection, and this is not always a popular alternative!

CONTINUATION OF THE TASK IN SUBSEQUENT LESSONS

The task then continues for a further two to five (or more) lessons, depending on your judgement and preference. We have suggested a six week structure below, but this is to be treated as a guide only.

We would recommend that performance is integrated throughout this process, for students to share work in progress with each other. This may be one or two groups every week, or you may choose to have an interim lesson during this process where each group performs to the rest of the class with the class feeding back on the performance. Alternatively, or additionally, you may regularly video/audio record and play back students' work so they can assess their own progress.

At the start of each lesson, you may choose to remind students of the task and of the ground rules. However, students can express frustration if they are not able to get on with the practical work straightaway.

OPTIONAL OUT-OF-HOURS LINK

Students often want access to practice/rehearsal spaces outside of lesson time to work on their songs during this project. Making spaces available to students, as well as scheduling in coaching sessions from your guitar, percussion, keyboard, vocal, etc peripatetic teachers can provide an incentive for students to stay behind after lesson/school time and continue with their work.

REVISITING THIS STAGE

Some schools choose to revisit In at the Deep End at other points during the school year. This can help students and teachers to see how their skills and knowledge have developed, and gives an opportunity for students to revisit learning their own music. Often students' choice of music broadens at this point. It is generally recommended that revisiting this stage should happen over a shorter time period (three weeks for example).

IN AT THE DEEP END

PROJECT SNAPSHOT

Lesson	Content
1	• Introduction to the informal learning model *(5 mins)* • Class discussion of how popular musicians learn *(10 mins)* • Explanation of task *(5 mins)* • Students group themselves into friendship groups, move into practice spaces and start discussing their song choice *(35 mins)* • Students feed back to class on possible group song choices *(5 mins)*
2	• Reiterate ground rules and task *(5 mins)* • Students carry on selecting their songs, and start choosing instruments when a song has been chosen *(50 mins)* • Feedback to class on group song choices and on what challenges students feel lie ahead *(5 mins)*
3	• Reiterate ground rules and task *(5 mins)* • Students work in friendship groups on their song choice *(45 mins)* • Ask one group to perform work in progress or have performances in practice spaces with the 'audience' moving round (as discussed in the initial guidance). Rest of class to feed back on the performance *(10 mins)*
4	• Reiterate ground rules and task *(5 mins)* • Students work in friendship groups on their song choice *(25 – 45 mins)* • Ask one group to perform work in progress and class to feedback *(10 – 30 mins)*
5	• Reiterate ground rules and task, tell students they will be recorded or will perform next lesson *(5 mins)* • Students work in friendship groups on their song choice *(50 mins)* • Feedback to class on how groups feeling they are progressing *(5 mins)*
6	• Reiterate ground rules and task, remind students they will be recorded or will perform today *(5 mins)* • Students work in friendship groups on their song choice *(25 mins)* • Group performances/videoing/class feedback/evaluation *(30 mins)*

Modelling Aural Learning

Having been dropped into the 'deep end', students are now given more guidance and structure through a broken-down 'musical model' of a song.

This involves giving students a CD which contains:

- The instrumental and vocal versions of a complete song

- A variety of riffs and/or rhythms played separately and in combination

The song chosen for this project should be in a popular style that students feel familiar with and can identify with – even if they do not necessarily know or even like the song.

This project also involves making some structured guidance about the song available to the students – for example a worksheet containing the note names of the riffs, guitar tablature, drum rhythms etc.

SONG CHOICE

The Musical Futures website (**www.musicalfutures.org.uk/modelling+aural+learning**) has the following broken-down songs and accompanying resources available for free download:

- *Word Up* (Cameo – this was the song used in the original informal learning model pilot)

- *Use Somebody* (Kings of Leon)

- *Hallelujah* (Leona Lewis version)

The reasons these particular songs have been chosen is because of the layers of riffs that are present. However we would strongly encourage teachers to take this concept and adapt it to any song or piece of music that they feel is appropriate for their students.

Choosing appropriate songs for Musical Futures projects requires careful consideration. If you are choosing a song to break-down for your students to work on, the following provides some guidance for doing this:

- Key: Is the original key of the recording good for the instruments your students will be using?

- Chord changes and sequences: Are the chord changes easy to follow? It can help to choose a song in which the chords don't change too quickly (for example once in a bar, or every other bar) or have a tricky harmonic rhythm

MODELLING AURAL LEARNING

○ Meter and tempo: It is a distinct advantage that the vast majority of contemporary songs are in 4/4 – songs in 3/4 or 6/8 can work but might need extra guidance. Medium tempo songs work well, either very slow or very fast are hard for drummers and could be difficult for other instrumentalists

○ Groove: Songs which feature clearly discernible grooves without too much variety or syncopation are preferable. Many rock and dance tracks are at medium tempos but feature complex syncopation, drum fills and variation which can be confusing

○ Melody: Some songs depend on an idiosyncratic performance style which can be difficult to follow. This extends to melodic shape and rhythm. As a general rule it helps if the song can be easily sung without any accompaniment. Large interval leaps and heavily embellished melody lines, melodies sung in falsetto or unusual vocal ranges can all be unhelpful

○ Instrumentation: Are there clearly discernible parts that can easily be replicated by beginner instrumentalists? If the texture is too thick, harmony can be difficult to follow, equally if the song is based around an intricate riff, beginner players can feel daunted

○ Do students like the song? Any song you choose is unlikely to be universally loved, but if the majority of students are enthused they will be more inclined to apply themselves to the project. Your experience of having completed In at the Deep End should give an indication of their tastes and developing skills

INFORMAL LEARNING PRINCIPLES

The key principles of informal learning for Modelling Aural Learning are:

○ Learning by listening and copying recordings

○ Learning with friends

Although the principle of learning music of their own choice is not followed in this part of the project, nonetheless the music is in a style that is familiar to most students.

The principle of personal, self-directed learning is also not applied so thoroughly here, since the CD/MP3, and other optional resource material such as note names and guitar tablature provides structured guidance. However, the role of the teacher, after the introductory parts of lessons, continues to be that of an observer, guide and advisor, rather than an instructor.

The principle of the integration of listening, performing, composing and improvising is brought into play slightly more than the In at the Deep End project. Students tend to show more signs of composing and/or improvising during this project, and any such practices should be encouraged.

TECHNOLOGY TIP
Consider uploading your chosen tracks to the projects section of NUMU (www.numu.org.uk) for students to download onto their phones/MP3 players/iPods. Student's performances can also be uploaded at the end of the project, allowing them to evaluate their own and each others' work, as well as using the blog feature to keep online records of progress. If you type 'Word Up' into the Artist/Title search on the NUMU homepage, there are various examples of student performances of the Cameo track.

PREPARATION

Visit the Musical Futures website (**www.musicalfutures.org.uk/ modelling+aural+learning**) and decide upon one set of tracks to download, or break down a song yourself. Familiarise yourself thoroughly with the music you are going to provide your students with, as well as the broken-down CD tracks and any additional resource material (all available on the website).

You will need to:

- Download and make copies of the chosen song and broken down parts per group of students. It is advisable to make a few spares in case of loss or damage
- Make enough copies of any extra resource material you are using (note-names, tablature, etc) for each individual student
- Alternatively, create your own broken-down song and resource materials

RESOURCES

- CD/MP3 containing complete song plus broken down riffs, one copy per group
- Guidance worksheets for students of note names, guitar tablature, etc (if using)
- CD/MP3 players/iPods with speakers, one per group
- Practice spaces, one per group
- Range of instruments – ideally of a typical 'band' set up (drums, guitar, bass, keyboards, microphones), and/or acoustic instruments, classroom percussion, and ideally access to ICT for students wanting to create music electronically

DISCUSSION, EXPLANATION AND DEMONSTRATION

Begin the first lesson with a class discussion and demonstration session.

- Explain to students that they will still be copying music from a CD, but that this time there is help given on the CD itself and on the accompanying resource material
- Play the class an extract of the complete song
- Explain that the riffs have been broken down on the CD, going from easy to difficult
- Play a selection of the riffs on the CD
- Call attention to the note-name and tablature guidance sheets (if using), explain and demonstrate how they relate to the CD tracks
- Model how to play different riffs on a keyboard, guitar etc, showing how they can be combined
- Indicate some parts which are easier to play, and some which are more difficult

MODELLING AURAL LEARNING

- If possible, ask one or two students to demonstrate different riffs to the rest of the class
- Play along with those students to model how the riffs can be combined within a band

Through such activities, explain and demonstrate to students that:

- The task is to copy and play along with the riffs on their chosen instruments, using the CD/MP3/iPod and the worksheets as guides
- It is best to start with the easier riffs first
- Some riffs can be combined to form harmonies, and some work well as bass lines
- Explain that students can play without the CD or can play along with any of the tracks on the CD
- Each group should aim to make up their own version of the song by putting the riffs together, and adding new riffs if desired

It should also be explained that, as before:

- Teachers will at first stand back, observe and diagnose, then guide, suggest and model
- Teachers will try to take on students' perspectives and help students to achieve the objectives that they set for themselves
- Students must continue to follow the ground rules concerning the norms of behaviour expected by the individual teacher, the department and the school

GETTING STARTED

Following the discussion/demonstration:

- Ask students to organise themselves into friendship groups
- Students then are instructed to take their CDs/MP3s and a CD/MP3 player/iPod into a practice space and start listening to the music
- Students select instruments and begin copying and putting together the riffs
- Either alert students to the availability of the guidance sheets (if using), or distribute these at the beginning of each lesson

CONTINUATION OF THE TASK IN SUBSEQUENT LESSONS

The task then continues for up to five lessons, depending on your judgement and preference. As with In at the Deep End, it is recommended that group performances are integrated regularly into the process.

At the start of each lesson, you may choose to remind students of the task and of the ground rules, or alternatively encourage students to get on with the practical work straightaway.

We have suggested a six-week structure below, but this is to be treated as a guide only.

OPTIONAL INTERIM LESSON

You might like to place an interim, more formal lesson at some stage within the early part of this project.

This could involve a peripatetic teacher, especially one with guitar and/or drum skills, giving students a more structured workshop on the use of the instruments, and where relevant how to read tablature and/or drum notation.

Such an approach would be particularly helpful where instruments that have not previously been familiar to the students are being used.

PROJECT SNAPSHOT

Lesson	Content
1	• Introduction to and explanation of the task *(5 mins)* • Modelling and demonstration session of how to use the tracks on the CD *(20 mins)* • Students group themselves into friendship groups and start to listen to the CD, begin to choose instruments and to find pitches on the instruments *(30 mins)* • Feedback to class *(5 mins)*
2	• Reiterate ground rules and task *(5 mins)* • Students choose instruments and start to work out riffs, and put them together in their groups *(50 mins)* • Feedback to the class on what challenges students feel lie ahead *(5 mins)*
3	• Optional interim skills-building workshop
4	• Reiterate ground rules and task *(5 mins)* • Students work in friendship groups on the song *(45 mins)* • Ask one group to perform work in progress, even if just a riff or a rhythm or have performances in practice spaces with 'audience' moving round (as discussed in the initial guidance). Rest of the class to feedback on performance *(10 mins)*
5	• Reiterate ground rules and task, tell students they will be recorded or will perform next lesson *(5 mins)* • Students work in friendship groups on their song choice *(45 mins)* • Ask one group to perform work in progress, or have performances in practice spaces with 'audience' moving round, and the class to feedback *(10 mins)*
6	• Reiterate ground rules and task, remind students they will be recorded or will perform today *(5 mins)* • Students work in friendship groups on the song *(25 mins)* • Group performances/videoing/class feedback/evaluation *(30 mins)*

Informal Composing

Students now move into creating their own music. Implicitly they build on what they have learned through listening and copying in earlier parts of the informal learning model. This replicates the way that popular musicians begin creating music by spontaneously basing their own ideas upon what they have learnt through listening and copying other music.

Students may initially attempt this task on their own, with little structured guidance. However, you may wish to consider building in structured advice and guidance taken from the world of popular music within or beyond the school. This can help students to understand how music is put together.

INFORMAL LEARNING PRINCIPLES

The key principles of informal learning for Informal Composing are:

- Learning music that students choose, like and identify with
- Learning with friends
- Personal, self-directed learning
- Integration of listening, performing, improvising and composing

The principle of learning by listening and copying recordings is not stressed in this project. However previous experiences of learning by listening and copying music inevitably inform students' approaches.

GUIDE TO SONGWRITING

You may find the Guide to Songwriting (page 101) provides a useful point of reference. This is designed to provide teachers and students with some hints and tips for writing songs. We would recommend that if you do integrate this advice into this project, you convey the advice to your students as and when they require it. You might also consider having an interim lesson on composing/songwriting techniques to support your students.

PREPARATION

- Familiarise yourself with the songwriting guide (if using)
- If a songwriting workshop is to be organised (see page 156), liaise either with visiting musicians or an existing band within the school, and set up the workshop

TECHNOLOGY TIP

Music software from entry-level packages to pro audio can be used to record ideas, and produce backing tracks for songs and instrumental compositions. They are particularly well suited to producing convincing rhythm tracks for dance compositions (from R 'n' B and grime to dubstep). It can also be helpful to use computer-based music software to create rhythm tracks, particularly in dance music styles. Furthermore, there are many websites that will allow students to download samples, which students may use to keep their productions sounding fresh and current.

RESOURCES

- Practice spaces, one per small group
- Range of instruments – ideally of a typical 'band' set up (drums, guitar, bass, keyboards, microphones), and/or acoustic instruments, classroom percussion; and ideally access to ICT for students wanting to create music electronically
- Songwriting guide (if using)
- Band of professional musicians or older students (if using)

DISCUSSION AND EXPLANATION

Begin the first lesson with a class discussion.

- Explain that students will now compose their own music
- They may compose either a song or an instrumental piece
- If setting lyrics, they may write their own, or adopt and adapt existing lyrics
- As a starting point, students may like to jam on musical riffs and ideas that they have already worked on through the listening and copying exercises

It should also be explained that:

- Teachers will at first stand back, observe and diagnose, then guide, suggest and model
- Teachers will try to take on students' perspectives and help students to achieve the objectives that they set for themselves
- Students must continue to follow the ground rules concerning the norms of behaviour expected by the individual teacher, the department and the school

GETTING STARTED

- Ask students to organise themselves into friendship groups
- Students are then instructed to go into practice spaces and start jamming/composing around their own musical ideas

INFORMAL COMPOSING

CONTINUATION OF THE TASK IN SUBSEQUENT LESSONS

After the initial lesson, we recommend students work on their own composing/songwriting ideas for a further two lessons before receiving more structured guidance which may consist of you:

- Bringing musicians into the classroom to model composing/songwriting for the students (see below)
- Running an interim lesson on songwriting techniques

Following this input of guidance and advice, allow students to continue working on and refining their own composing/songwriting ideas for a further two/three lessons (depending on your judgment and preference).

As with the earlier projects, it is recommended that group performances are integrated regularly into the process.

At the start of each lesson, you may choose to remind students of the task and of the ground rules, or alternatively to encourage students to get on with the practical work.

We have suggested a six-week structure below, but this is to be treated as a guide only.

MODELLING COMPOSING

Where possible, bringing popular musicians into the classroom – whether from outside the school or within the school community – to perform and demonstrate songwriting and composing to students can be highly beneficial in terms of giving students ideas, and engaging with live music and other musicians' perspectives. It also allows students to learn by watching more experienced musicians perform. If this is something that can be arranged, visiting musicians should be briefed to:

- Play one or more songs/pieces that they have written themselves
- Take the music apart – for example by playing the bass line, melody, chords and drum parts separately
- Stress the importance of communicating within a group situation and listening to each others' ideas
- Talk in non-technical terms about how a song came into being
- Answer any questions that the students have
- Work with the students on their own songwriting, giving them advice where appropriate

In many schools, teachers use older 'bands' of students in this role, or in some cases bands of same-age students. This can work particularly well as students generally respond well to peers, and they can act as positive role models. If you are going to engage a band of students to do this, you may need to help them with introducing their music and talking about how they constructed it, as while some students are very confident performers they can find discussing their own music more challenging.

OPTIONAL OUT-OF-HOURS LINK

Consider establishing a songwriting club, ideally with a music technology link, for budding songwriters to continue with their work. The *Writers Unblocked* resource developed by the Leeds pathfinders, gives some ideas for developing songwriting as an extra-curricular activity. Download it from **www.musicalfutures.org.uk/songwriting**.

PROJECT SNAPSHOT

Lesson	Content
1	• Introduction to and explanation of the task *(10 mins)* • Optional description of basic songwriting techniques *(30 mins)* • Students group themselves into friendship groups and start to compose collaboratively *(20 mins)*
2	• Reiterate ground rules and task *(5 mins)* • Students continue working in groups on their own music *(40 mins)* • Ask one group to perform work in progress, even if just a riff or a rhythm. Rest of class to feedback *(10 mins)* • Class to feedback on their progress *(5 mins)*

3	• Workshop session either with visiting musicians or with older band from the school. Session to include:
	  → Demonstration by band of songs they have written
	  → Explanation of how they wrote their own music
	  → Questions and answers from the rest of the class
	  → Class breaks into friendship groups and continue with own compositions, whilst musicians go round assisting students with their own work

4	• Reiterate ground rules and task, and recap on what students learnt from the workshop session *(10 mins)* • Students work in friendship groups on the composing task *(40 mins)* • Ask one group to perform work in progress, even if just a riff or a rhythm, or have performances in practice spaces with 'audience' moving round. Rest of class to feedback on performance *(10 mins)*
5	• Reiterate ground rules and task, tell students they will be recorded or will perform next lesson *(5 mins)* • Students work in friendship groups on the composing task *(45 mins)* • Ask one group to perform work in progress and class to feedback *(10 mins)*
6	• Reiterate ground rules and task, remind students they will be recorded or will perform today *(5 mins)* • Students work in friendship groups on the composing task *(25 mins)* • Group performances/videoing/class feedback/evaluation *(30 mins)*

Informal Learning with Other Musics

This project draws on the practice of learning by listening and copying, but using music that may lie outside students' immediate choice, and might not be familiar to them. The rationale is to continue to adopt informal learning practices, but drawing students away from what they already know and into the wider world of music.

This project is structured into two sections:

- Into the Deep End with Other Musics
- Modelling Other Musics

You may choose to follow both sections in sequence, or to just select one or the other.

Resources in classical music, and world fusion music are available for download from **www.musicalfutures.org.uk/informal+learning+and+other+musics**. However teachers may adapt this concept to music from any time or place.

Many students have classical instrumental lessons and enjoy playing classical music alone and in a variety of bands and orchestras. But even for these students, classical music is rarely listened to as part of their leisure time, and students often have few positive things to say about classical music. Whether because of peer pressure, or genuine issues of taste and identity, classical music is a problem area for most students of this age group.

Therefore classical music, and other musics (for example the world fusion pieces included online) are very much a part of the informal learning model, by continuing to adopt learning methodologies that students are by now likely to feel familiar with, and by introducing other musics in this context.

FURTHER READING

Professor Lucy Green's publication *Music, Informal Learning and the School* (Ashgate, 2008) provides a full analysis of the ways students responded to classical music during the pilot phase of Musical Futures.

NOTE CONCERNING PROJECT ORDER

You may prefer firstly to implement the Modelling Other Musics project (page 161), followed by Into the Deep End With Other Musics – depending on your judgment and preference. If just one of these two projects is to be followed, we recommend Modelling Other Musics, as it gives more guidance and structure to help pupils approach unfamiliar music.

Into the Deep End with Other Musics

NOTE

This isn't a project about music and advertising, instead it is drawing on pre-existing music used for TV advertisements as the starting point for informal learning. The reason for this is that the task of aural copying is more approachable if the music is familiar; later on students tackle music that is unlikely to be familiar to them.

As with In at the Deep End (see page 144), students are dropped into the deep end in this project. They are given a CD/MP3 containing music that has appeared on television advertisements, but which isn't popular music. However while this music may be outside students' immediate choice, they may be familiar with the music through hearing it on the television. They are asked to copy the music aurally from a CD/MP3, and work in friendship groups with their own choice of instruments.

INFORMAL LEARNING PRINCIPLES

The key principles of informal learning for Into the Deep End with Other Music are:

- Learning by listening and copying recordings
- Learning with friends
- Personal, self-directed learning without structured guidance

The principle of learning music that students choose, like and identify with is challenged here. The principle of integrating listening, performing, improvising and composing is not stressed in this stage, but tends to be an outcome of the fact that students 'make the music their own', and engage in a certain amount of improvising and composing.

PREPARATION

Source a number of tracks that have been used in recent television advertisements, and which are not popular musics, using online sites such as www.whatsthattune.co.uk or www.soundsfamiliar.info. Prepare a CD/MP3 for students of up to five tracks for them to copy. The Musical Futures website (www.musicalfutures.org.uk/informal+learning+and+other+musics) contains some suggestions for possible tracks that are current at the time of publication.

RESOURCES

- Compile CD/MP3s of music used in television advertisements, one per group
- CD/MP3 players/iPods, one per group
- Practice spaces, one per group
- Range of instruments – ideally of a typical 'band' set up (drums, guitar, bass, keyboards, microphones), and/or acoustic instruments, classroom percussion, and ideally access to ICT for students wanting to create music electronically

INFORMAL LEARNING WITH OTHER MUSICS

DISCUSSION AND EXPLANATION

Begin the project by explaining:

- Students will copy music aurally from a CD/MP3

- However, this time students will not be bringing in their own music, but instead must choose one of the pieces from the CD/MP3 provided

- Explain that the music is taken from advertisements – if desired, explain what kind of music it is, and why it will be helpful for students to gain some familiarity with this music; for example they will begin to understand and appreciate it more

It should also be explained that, as before:

- Teachers will at first stand back, observe and diagnose, then guide, suggest and model

- Teachers will try to take on students' perspectives and help students to achieve the objectives that they set for themselves

- Students must continue to follow the ground rules concerning the norms of behaviour expected by the individual teacher, the department and the school

GETTING STARTED

- Ask students to organise themselves into friendship groups

- Instruct students to take their CDs/MP3s and a CD/MP3 player/iPod into a practice space, start listening to the music, and to select one track to copy

- Explain that students may select any instruments they wish; and that they do not have to attempt to copy the exact sounds on the recording. For example, if there is singing but there is no vocalist in the group, the voice could be copied using a synthesiser or any other instrument. Also, instruments such as drums and percussion can be added

- Explain that students are free to make the music their own, by arranging it in whatever way suits their group, including adding drum-beats if desired. In our experience students find the concept of arranging music for different forces new and hard to grasp, so it may be worth demonstrating how a piece written for certain instruments can be arranged for different ones. In particular, students may wish to continue to use percussion in their arrangements; this can be helpful to keep them in time and should be encouraged as an aspect of arranging the music

- Proceed into small groups and begin

CONTINUATION OF THE TASK IN SUBSEQUENT LESSONS

The task can then either continue for two or three lessons, to be followed by the second part of this project, or for longer, depending on your judgment or preference.

At the start of each lesson, you may choose to remind students of the task and of the ground rules. However, students can express frustration if they are not able to get on with the practical work straightaway.

As with the earlier projects, it is recommended that group performances are integrated regularly into the process.

Modelling Other Musics

This section introduces students to music that is likely to be less familiar to them, but offers more structure and guidance. It operates in a similar way to Modelling Aural Learning (see page 149), in that each piece of music is broken down into simplified, separate audio tracks so that the melody and bass can be heard, copied and played along with separately.

INFORMAL LEARNING PRINCIPLES

The key principles of informal learning for Modelling Other Musics are:

- Learning by listening and copying recordings
- Learning with friends

The principle of learning music that students choose, like and identify with is particularly challenged in this project. The principle of personal, self-directed learning without structured guidance is not emphasised in this stage, as there is guidance through the CD tracks. However, the role of the teacher continues to be that of an observer, guide and adviser, rather than an instructor. The principle of integrating listening, performing, improvising and composing is not stressed here, but tends to be an outcome of the fact that students make the music their own, and engage in a certain amount of improvising and composing.

PREPARATION

Visit the Musical Futures website (**www.musicalfutures.org.uk/ informal+learning+and+other+musics**) and decide upon which 'sets' of tracks to download and make copies for your students. You may choose to provide students with a CD just containing classical music, just containing world fusion music, or containing a mixture of both. Alternatively you may choose to develop your own resources using music from any time and place.

The Musical Futures website contains the following material:

- Classical music tracks:
    - → Beethoven: *Für Elise*
    - → Mozart: *Eine Kleine Nachtmusik* (1st movt opening)
    - → Clara Schumann: *Piano Trio* (1st movt opening)
    - → Handel: *Flute Sonata Op. 1, no. 5* (Minuet)
    - → Brahms: *Symphony no. 1* (4th movt theme)
    - → Bach: *Anna Magdalena Notebook* (Minuet in G minor)
    - → Elizabeth Jacquet de la Guerre: *Sonata in D* (Allegro)
    - → Borodin: *Polovtsian Dance no. 5* (opening)

INFORMAL LEARNING WITH OTHER MUSICS

- World fusion tracks:
  - → Anakhi: *Lok Boliyan* (bhangra)
  - → Golden Sounds Band/Rama Issa: *Maisha* (Kenyan)
  - → Little Grasscals: *Nine Pound Hammer* (bluegrass)

RESOURCES

- CD/MP3 containing complete song/piece plus broken down material of your chosen song/pieces, one copy per group
- CD/MP3 players/iPods, one per group
- Practice spaces, one per group
- Range of instruments – ideally of a typical 'band' set up (drums, guitar, bass, keyboards, microphones), and/or acoustic instruments, classroom percussion, and ideally access to ICT for students wanting to create music electronically

DISCUSSION, EXPLANATION AND DEMONSTRATION

Begin the project as follows:

- Explain that students will aurally copy some more music, but this time with guidance from the CD/MP3
- Explain that the CD/MP3 has a number of different pieces to choose from, and that each piece is also broken down into separate tracks including a simplified version and separate melody and bass parts
- Listen as a class to short extracts of some of the original pieces, and extracts of the simplified versions and individual melody or bass parts
- Indicate some parts which are easier to play, and some which are more difficult
- Demonstrate a selection of the parts on an instrument
- Explain that students are free to make the music their own, by arranging it in whatever way suits their group.

In our experience students find the concept of arranging music for different forces new and hard to grasp, so it may be worth demonstrating how a piece written for certain instruments can be arranged for different ones. In particular, many students may wish to continue to use percussion in their arrangements; this can be helpful to keep them in time and should be encouraged as an aspect of arranging the music.

It should also be explained that, as before:

- Teachers will at first stand back, observe and diagnose, then guide, suggest and model
- Teachers will try to take on students' perspectives and help students to achieve the objectives that they set for themselves.
- Students must continue to follow the ground rules concerning the norms of behaviour expected by the individual teacher, the department and the school

GETTING STARTED

- Ask students to organise themselves into friendship groups
- Students then are instructed to take their CDs/MP3s and a CD/MP3 player/iPod into a practice space, start listening to the music and select which piece they are going to work on
- Students select instruments and begin copying and putting together their own version of the piece
- Proceed into small groups and begin

CONTINUATION OF THE TASK IN SUBSEQUENT LESSONS

As with earlier projects, it is recommended that group performances are integrated regularly into the process.

At the start of each lesson, you may choose to remind students of the task and of the ground rules, or alternatively to encourage students to get on with the practical work.

We have suggested a six-week structure below, but this is to be treated as a guide only.

PROJECT SNAPSHOT

Lesson	Content
1	• Introduction to and explanation of the 'Into the Deep End with Other Musics' task *(5 mins)* • Students group themselves into friendship groups; listen to the CD; choose a piece to copy/arrange; choose instruments *(50 mins)* • Feedback to class *(5 mins)*
2	• Reiterate ground rules and task *(5 mins)* • Students work in friendship groups on their song choice *(55 mins)*
3	• Reiterate ground rules and task *(5 mins)* • Students work in friendship groups on their song choice *(45 mins)* • Ask one or two groups to perform work in progress. Rest of class to feedback on performance *(10 mins)*
4	• Introduction to and explanation of the 'Modelling Other Musics' task *(5 mins)* • Modelling and demonstration session of how to use the tracks on the CD *(20 mins)* • Students group themselves into friendship groups and start to listen to the CD *(30 mins)* • Feedback to class *(5 mins)*
5	• Reiterate ground rules and task *(5 mins)* • Students work in friendship groups on their song choice *(55 mins)*
6	• Reiterate ground rules and task, remind students they will be recorded or will perform today *(5 mins)* • Students work in friendship groups on their song *(25 mins)* • Group performances/videoing/class feedback/evaluation *(30 mins)*

Case Study: Oasis Academy Lord's Hill

Oasis Academy Lord's Hill is a new academy specialising in Arts with Business and Enterprise catering for 11–16 year olds, with 880 students. It is situated in an area of deprivation in Southampton, with 38% of students on the Special Educational Needs register. The new Academy opened in September 2008 following the reorganisation of secondary schools in Southampton by the Local Authority. The Academy comprises the staff and students of two neighbouring predecessor schools. Only one of the predecessor schools employed Musical Futures (all historical information relates to that school) and the other had no music teacher at all for two years prior to the opening of the Academy. The resulting percentage numbers of students opting for music in 2008/9 has gone down, as has the percentage of students taking instrumental/vocal tuition. The waiting list for tuition now is large and is expected to increase peripatetic hours next year to meet demand.

- Typical class size: 22

- % of students involved in instrumental/vocal tuition: over 14% (projected to be more than 20% next year)

- % of students taking KS4 music: 13%

- % of students involved in extra-curricular music projects: 30%

OASIS ACADEMY AND MUSICAL FUTURES

The Head of Music started exploring Musical Futures in one of the Academy's predecessor schools in 2006. The new Academy has created a curricular environment in which the Musical Futures informal learning approach has been re-developed. Music is delivered as part of the Opening Minds competency-based curriculum in Year 7. Students may elect to take music after Year 8, and may re-choose at the end of Year 9.

Paul Ibbott, Head of Music at Oasis Academy Lord's Hill, explains their approach to Musical Futures.

WHY MUSICAL FUTURES?

"Music at my school has had a difficult history. When I joined the school, there had been no music teacher for two years. Building a new department from scratch was a challenge I relished and I set about trying to recreate the fairly successful department from my previous school. In some respects my work was successful. Students often said music was their favourite subject, but this wasn't translated into good GCSE candidates and Key Stage 4 attainment seemed to reach a low plateau.

I attended a Musical Futures training day, where I realised that the attainment plateau was little to do with ability and everything to do with engagement – what I was offering was not really exciting the students. I also realised a blindingly obvious fact: I was not teaching music in the way I learnt music. Although I had a certain amount of classical training, the majority of what I knew about music was learnt in my mate's front room trying to emulate my favourite musicians, writing songs and arranging them for different instrumental groups – and I wasn't even aware I was learning. I learned through the experience and enjoyment of a relatively narrow field of music to then appreciate music on a wider scale. I appreciated different styles and traditions because I became knowledgeable about one. On the other hand, my students were being fed a wide range of styles and traditions which had little personal significance for them and which, with one or two exceptions, seemed to be dousing any spark of interest in studying music.

The Musical Futures training day gave me 'permission' to experiment and do something different, not for the sake of doing it differently, but because the informal approach chimed with my own experience. It was not just that I felt it appropriate for my students; it was as much about my own development as a teacher.

OASIS ACADEMY'S MUSICAL FUTURES APPROACH

I started the informal learning model in September 2006, despite having a lack of practice rooms and no additional available staff. I was fortunate in having a supportive senior management team who, in spite of misgivings about unsupervised students, facilitated the implementation by allowing the use of a variety of cupboards and junk rooms around the school.

CASE STUDY: OASIS ACADEMY LORD'S HILL

One or two teachers expressed concern about unsupervised students 'doing whatever they want' around the school and saw any behaviour problems that arose as an obvious consequence of the situation and an argument against my method of organisation. In reality, behaviour problems involved exactly the same students as would cause difficulties in regular classes. Situations never escalated beyond that which could be dealt with by the teacher – an improvement over the previous year!

I opened my first Musical Futures lessons by explaining to students that while I was still 'Sir', a new relationship was going to develop whereby the students themselves would identify what they wanted to learn, and I would give them help as and when they asked for it.

The students were given their first task – to get into friendship groups and choose a song that they would like to try to copy (see In at the Deep End, page 144). Finding a group that 'worked' took weeks with some individuals, and we had some problems with song choice – they had to negotiate with their band members to find a song they all wanted to do. Nevertheless, the students remained enthusiastically focussed on the task even though it seemed to me that nothing was being achieved.

At the end of the unit I gave all Year 9 students a questionnaire about Musical Futures so far. Nearly all students said they preferred Musical Futures lessons to previous lessons and felt they had made progress in learning instruments. Many students were pleased to be trusted to work unsupervised, and identified that learning how to get on in groups was an important skill being developed. The few (all girls) who did not enjoy Musical Futures lessons said that they did not want to learn instruments or sing.

I was expecting the second unit (Modelling Aural Learning, see page 149), to go badly because the song we used (*Word Up* by Cameo) was not exactly up-to-date. In fact the students recognised the song and were happy to have a go. At the end of the unit, nearly all students performed. The change occurred because, according to them, they felt more confident and practised more. The simplicity of the song, additional resources, and the fact they didn't have to choose a song, were also important factors. Students understood that in order to succeed, they could choose simpler songs and search for tab and lyrics on the Internet. Had I explained this at the beginning of term, I am sure I would still be nagging them to resource their work. Because students learned this for themselves, they developed their own culture of printing lyrics, tab and burning CDs.

We then revisited In at the Deep End, which saw students working in a focused way making creative, musical decisions beyond simply learning to play the notes – they were arranging the songs, simplifying parts, even composing their own material. Students still struggled to make a good ensemble sound, but they could hear themselves making progress.

A lesson was observed by my senior management team around this time and the observation noted the progress in emotional literacy made by students with special needs, quite apart from the engagement and attainment. It was noted that students were setting their own objectives (although they were not formalised) and assessing their progress against their own ideas of what success was. I was continuing to try to assess against National Curriculum levels, but students were more interested

CASE STUDY: OASIS ACADEMY LORD'S HILL

in whether it sounded good, and they knew that without my saying so. They still wanted me to give my assessment of their work but they wanted to validate their own opinions and sometimes would try to justify their own view where it differed from mine.

The unit incorporating classical music (Informal Learning with Other Musics, see page 158) did not last longer than a week, as students were simply not interested. However during the following year, students who had been through Musical Futures started voluntarily experimenting with classical ideas for inspiration and enjoyed listening to popular classics, appreciating their skill, complexity and artistry. The teacher/student interactions in respect to orchestral works, structure, colour and virtuosity were among the most positive and musical I have ever experienced as a teacher.

Attainment across the cohort was difficult to analyse and compare with previous years. In some respects students had clearly outperformed previous groups: instrumental and performing skills were more widespread and of a higher average standard. Set against this was a lack of knowledge and experience of a wider range of musical traditions and less opportunity to demonstrate and develop composition skills. In the light of subsequent Key Stage 4 results, it might be true to say that what Musical Futures lacks in breadth, it more than makes up for in depth. The engagement of students and ignition of musical passion in more musically-able students has been evident.

Trying Musical Futures for a second year enabled me to direct some peripatetic resources into the classes. The equipment had been well looked after by the students and required only minor repairs. I repeated the successful units and dropped those which did not work. On reflection, this may have been a mistake since I was removing opportunities for work to develop in the directions of classical and world music based on my preconceptions of what the students would want rather than their expressed wishes. To my surprise, *Word Up* fell flat. Students wanted to cover *Seven Nation Army* instead, so some quick resources were developed to accommodate this.

At the end of my first year of Musical Futures I realised that the GCSE course I was offering was simply not going to deliver what students wanted from music lessons – I had unsuccessful GCSE results and students were losing interest in the course. I discovered the Rockschool suite of qualifications. After careful consideration and consultation with students and parents, I switched the GCSE course to Rockschool. This breathed life into my Year 11 group which achieved over 80% A*–C equivalent, with 30% A* equivalents. Rockschool, as a BTEC style qualification, dovetails very neatly into the learner-led ethos of Musical Futures. It allows students to build their qualification from a wide range of units according to their strengths and preferences. Currently, students may opt for music in Year 9 where I combine Musical Futures with a level 2 Rockschool unit.

I am now engaged in a pilot project with a feeder junior school which, after some initial skills development, aims to introduce Musical Futures to Year 5 pupils. Very early signs are encouraging and the school has asked for the project to be extended. I am also in the early planning stages of a project with the aim of re-introducing adults who used

CASE STUDY: OASIS ACADEMY LORD'S HILL

to play instruments to group music making. The approach taken may well depend on the wishes of the participants themselves, but will be greatly informed by the informal learning approach by providing an environment where people can learn together in groups.

RESOURCING MUSICAL FUTURES

Being committed to informal learning means resourcing the students' chosen learning pathway appropriately. I originally had some money ear-marked for ICT equipment, which I re-directed towards equipping Musical Futures with entry-level equipment – PA systems and microphones, guitars, basses, practice amps, and two electronic drum kits and smaller drum pad machines.

Having only one practice room, I was allowed to use a variety of small rooms spread around the school. This required a far greater degree of trust in the students than I was comfortable with. It also meant that a high proportion of a lesson was spent with unproductive walking between rooms. If students needed help, they would often come looking for me which meant they were wandering around the school building.

The music department has now moved onto a different site. There is an old but purpose-built music facility that enables all group work to take place in a small area. I was able to secure capital to spend on new equipment. Students are now beginning to see uses for ICT beyond effects pedals and MP3 recorders, so that is the plan for future investment.

TEACHING STYLES

The most important change has been the level of trust I place in the students to direct their own learning. I have learned that the important thing is to be flexible and to expect the unexpected. Informal learning is, almost by definition, unpredictable. There needs to be a continuous appraisal of progress and willingness to change direction, remembering that refinements that may work the first time are not guaranteed to work thereafter. There is no formula.

In the first year of implementation, there was a group of girls who, for a term and a half, had not really engaged with any instruments and did not want to sing. One day they showed some initiative and asked me if they could dance to a track instead. I told them no, because it was a music lesson. I immediately saw their faces drop and they disengaged completely. I never managed to recapture any enthusiasm from that group. Reflecting on this, I realised that the girls wanted to personalise their musical experience and could actually have gone on to develop musically through their preferred pathway. I resolved to become a 'yes man' from then on.

It has not always proved easy to maintain such an approach. One Year 10 band is currently creating its own original material. All except one of the seven band members are on the SEN register, three of them for behaviour. The band needs more supervision and attention than most, though the students often ask for musical input. Recently I was

CASE STUDY: OASIS ACADEMY LORD'S HILL

asked to help arrange their musical ideas and I took over. I thought I was taking their ideas and spreading them across the band quite cleverly; I differentiated the parts and maintained appropriate musical interest and challenge. We all worked hard for an entire morning and reached a point where all the students showed what I would call good progress. I was very proud of myself and suggested to colleagues that they visit the band in the afternoon to hear the group. After lunch the band came back and told me that the whole song, as we had practised it, was too slow, didn't have enough energy and was 'all wrong'. It felt like a personal attack – I had invested a lot in the song and they were criticising me. I then realised that my feelings pointed to the problem. I would not feel any personal offence had I not imposed my ideas on the work. I had taken the students down **my** pathway, not walked with them down theirs.

I am continually looking for ways to increase the level of trust. I hold tightly to the belief that students actually want to learn and I address off-task or disruptive behaviour by asking the students what they want to learn. This avoids confrontation and reinforces the positive relationship between teacher and student.

Students now complete formal individual lesson plans/reviews at the start and end of each lesson to set objectives, plan how to meet them, review progress and set targets for the next lesson. Initially I felt embarrassed about the idea of students setting their own objectives; it felt like a cop out. But as I read more about informal learning, I came to the belief that developing life-long, independent learning was the aim of teaching. The more I do for the students, the more they are dependent on me. One of the questions on the students' lesson plans is: 'How do I want the teacher to help me today?' Students plan my time as well as their own.

WIDER IMPACT

Musical Futures has helped make the department a more relaxed place. Paradoxically this also involves a stronger drive towards excellence in music making but this drive emanates from students rather than being imposed by the teacher. It has also helped to make the department a more 'cool' place to be and has enabled me to raise the profile of the department in the school because students are happier to perform to their peers. I am currently planning to start a project to encourage colleagues to look at learner-led, informal approaches across the curriculum.

ADVICE FOR OTHERS CONSIDERING MUSICAL FUTURES?

Many music departments, in particular those satisfied with their results, may wonder why they need Musical Futures at all. It is true that the original incentive for me was to try to turn my department around. Were my students achieving 50% A*–C at GCSE I might not have considered Musical Futures.

CASE STUDY: OASIS ACADEMY LORD'S HILL

However, the truth is that it is not about results but about the education of the young people entrusted to me. Once students experience Musical Futures, they do not want to go back to 'traditional' lessons. They value the responsibility and trust placed in them very highly indeed.

My advice to other teachers is:

- Read about informal learning and learner-directed learning
- Visit a school already utilising Musical Futures
- Give the students plenty of time
- Trust the students' desire to learn
- Always seek to facilitate, never impose
- Resource the department with good-quality equipment
- Get as much expert help into the classroom as you can
- Don't let a lack of space or money become excuses not to try Musical Futures
- Musical Futures may be a way of increasing Key Stage 4 uptake – if an appropriate course can be offered **"**

Oasis Academy Lord's Hill is a Musical Futures Champion School

SECTION 4
Organisation and Design

Developing Extra-curricular Provision

Music learning takes place in many different contexts (in school, after school, in youth and community settings, in homes, garages and online) and there is a growing acknowledgment of the benefits of a more holistic view of students' interests, needs and achievements. Getting the fullest picture of students' musical progression is best served by piecing together their experiences in formal (throughout the curriculum and instrumental tuition), non-formal (supervised work undertaken outside school hours), and informal (in their own time, without supervision) locations.

The essence of this guidance is to find ways of bringing together formal, non-formal and informal opportunities for learning in order to widen and deepen participation in extra-curricular provision. The process we detail here encourages schools and Music Services/other brokering agencies to work together to identify projects which could meet the personalised needs of all young people.

There is a need to move away from a 'one size fits all' approach towards one in which a young person's learning experience is better matched to their perceived needs and aspirations. It is also about the learner's active engagement in the process, helping them to:

- Reflect on and make choices about their aspirations and needs
- Make choices about their future
- Shape their learning experiences

You will no doubt already have a range of information about your students – from formal assessment records to more informal judgments and views, but it is likely that much of this information is based on what is seen and assessed as a result of work undertaken in the classroom.

Here we are concerned with adding to this knowledge base by beginning a dialogue with students, taking the opportunity to find out about their musical life outside school, and to link this with their formal learning experience in order to co-construct and agree an Individual Music Learning Plan (IMLP) with them.

RESOURCES

Personalising Extra-curricular Music Activities for 11–18 Year Olds, developed by the Leeds pathfinders, is available to download from **www.musicalfutures.org. uk/extra-curricular+provision**

DEVELOPING EXTRA-CURRICULAR PROVISION

NOTE

Many of the Musical Futures projects in this resource pack provide opportunities for diagnosing students' musical skills, experiences and interests, as well as potentially being run as extra-curricular projects themselves.

We would suggest that this is best done through a three-stage, circular process:

- **Stage 1**: Diagnose students' musical skills, previous experiences and future interests
- **Stage 2**: Plan projects according to identified needs and with appropriate partners (for example Music Services, community musicians and student leaders) – this encompasses curriculum, workforce development, and mentoring and coaching
- **Stage 3**: Review both project delivery and student achievement, so that new goals can be set – this involves Assessment for Learning, and advice and guidance

There is a danger, however, with any planning format that the arrangements 'over manage' the process. The format and processes for developing IMLPs should liberate learning rather than harness learners – that's why the initial diagnosis outlined below is described as a 'dialogue' – remembering always that the learner is central to the process. It is *their* IMLP, agreed with an adult who acts as a key advocate. Who this adult is (and as mentioned below, this does not necessarily always have to be the teacher) is likely to be informed by:

- The learner's preference – having an awareness of each student's relationship with the questioner, and knowing that who's asking the question and how it's asked will determine the honesty and quality of the response
- The time and skills required to stimulate and sustain the learner's engagement with the process

NOTE

The Ofsted report *Making More of Music* (available from **www.ofsted.gov.uk**) refers to how extra-curricular activities should reflect the interests and experiences of the students, rather than of the subject leaders: "Schools should analyse student involvement in extra-curricular work, and identify those students who would benefit most – musically and personally – from involvement in extra-curricular activity" (Ofsted).

Whoever undertakes this role would need to feedback to the teacher or the 'learning manager'. They will take the responsibility to plan appropriate support and to ensure that there are clear progression opportunities for all students, irrespective of their curricular choices.

It is important to stress that this couldn't, nor shouldn't, be undertaken by a solitary professional. Many Music Services, and other organisations such as MusicLeader and Youth Music Action Zones, support the varied pathways which students follow, and support the professionals who try to make sense of the journeys to enable students to be guided towards further progression.

The point of bringing together the formal, non-formal and informal in music learning is to bring the range of practitioners from those areas together to better understand each other's roles. Within schools, this could encompass learning mentors, teaching assistants, PGCE students, as well as music teachers and other subject staff. The opportunities provided within the Extended Schools programme make it possible to put together more coherent extra-curricular programmes of this sort, with schools being in a much stronger position to make closer links to the formal curriculum.

Young people require an exposure to a whole range of professional music expertise, and they need this in a variety of different contexts. Music Services and similar agencies are in a prime position to help them work to achieve this.

DEVELOPING EXTRA-CURRICULAR PROVISION

STAGE 1: DIAGNOSIS

The first step in this process is to listen to and observe individual responses and reactions to what is being offered in the classroom, and to take the opportunity to find out something of the musical life of students outside the school.

This may mean planning a lesson which gets the majority of students working quickly and independently (In at the Deep End, page 144, Band Instrumental Work, page 88 or Guide to Classroom Workshopping, page 47, may be good starting points), enabling either yourself or another adult to 'step back' and focus on a manageable number of students.

Below are some examples of questions used in previous Musical Futures projects that you may consider asking your students during their school music lessons, but you would no doubt wish to create your own:

- What are you enjoying most in music at the moment?
- Do you mainly listen to music at home, or do you also make your own music?
- Do you enjoy discussing music?
- Are there activities and experiences which you particularly enjoy or things that you would like to get better at?
- What does your school/college do well?
- What helps you in your music lessons? Why?
- What doesn't help you and why?

It's worth remembering that the aim, either through discussion or through questionnaires/evaluations, is to gauge students' readiness to learn rather than their current skill or ability and that the focus is on the students' musical experiences outside school and how much they feel that this links with their learning in school.

You then will need to interpret the responses which the students provide, seeking to measure their capacity for:

- Engagement in learning
- Responsibility for learning
- Independence in learning, with student control over learning
- Confidence in learning and their own abilities
- Maturity in relationships with staff and among peers, and how much responsibility are they (and the teacher) taking to co-construct the design of teaching and learning

The pamphlet *Supporting Young Musicians and Coordinating Musical Pathways* (David Price) discusses the out-of-hours curriculum created by the Leeds Musical Futures pathfinder, and identifies groups of typical participants as follows:

- **Refusers:** students with little inclination to engage with music other than as consumers
- **Waverers:** students who have an interest in music, but are not sure what they want to do, or how they want to participate
- **Explorers:** students who have some skills and confidence, but have not yet found the vehicle which matches their participatory preferences

NOTE

This pamphlet can be downloaded from www.musicalfutures.org.uk/c/pamphlets

DEVELOPING EXTRA-CURRICULAR PROVISION

○ **Directors:** students who already access a range of opportunities, and are developing performance and rehearsal skills

Questioning and supporting students through informal consultations might elicit a range of responses which could involve students being placed along the following continuum:

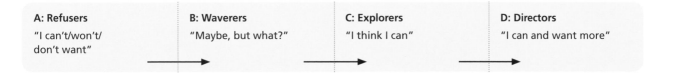

A: Refusers	B: Waverers	C: Explorers	D: Directors
"I can't/won't/ don't want"	"Maybe, but what?"	"I think I can"	"I can and want more"

However simplistic, this allows the learning manager to work towards a series of objectives which address students' position on this continuum. Within these four broad interpretations of response, a series of objectives might look like:

A	B	C	D
Engage, enjoy, excite. Students choose their own way in.	Build confidence and a sense of achievement.	Increase confidence, independence and a sense of achievement.	More independence, extending, deepening learning, clear sense of direction.

STAGE 2: PLANNING

Once you have agreed with your students which of the above categories they most identify with, the next stage is developing your extra-curricular offer, where the following questions become critical:

1) **What** is the most appropriate activity to achieve the objective? (for example projects which contain elements of authenticity, based within real-life parameters with credible end products (for example gigs, recording opportunities, etc)

2) **Who** is the most appropriate person to support the activity? (for example classroom teacher, peripatetic music tutor, community musician, older student)

3) **Where** might the activity take place? (for example in school, community venues, local recording studios, town centre performing venues, etc)

4) **When** might the activity take place? (for example during the school day, after school, at weekends, in the holidays?)

DEVELOPING EXTRA-CURRICULAR PROVISION

Based upon this process so far, you should then be able to work with students to co-construct an informal curriculum of projects, or pathways, which offer a number of progression points, according to students' readiness to learn and their musical development.

The table opposite gives some general ideas (based on past Musical Futures experiences) for different types of extra-curricular provision, who it might appeal to, and what sort of resources you may need to consider.

NOTE

A list of specific projects isn't given here, as the aim of this exercise is to create projects that meet the needs of your students. The first edition teacher resource pack outlines the projects the Musical Futures Leeds pathfinder team implemented during the pathfinder years.

SECTION 4: ORGANISATION AND DESIGN

DEVELOPING EXTRA-CURRICULAR PROVISION

Target group	Project type	Project description	Potential benefits	People	Resources	Potential cost
A	Music portfolio.	A self-led student record of engagement; either accredited in house and/or used to contribute to Arts Award (www.artsaward.org.uk).	• All areas of student engagement, participation and progression is logged, acknowledged and accredited • Can act as a focus for young people to connect areas of their musical engagement	Music teacher or learning mentor, peripatetic teacher or youth leader.	A physical portfolio for students. See *Build Your Own Portfolio* materials, available from www.musicalfutures.org.uk/extra-curricular+provision	None if built into a pre-existing activity or lesson.
A	Music taster workshop sessions.	Arrange a number of taster sessions in different musical styles and genres for young people, as a means of establishing what extra-curricular work might be successful and might appeal to students. This could be hosted in school lessons, as part of an activities week, or as a series of after-school taster sessions. The type of sessions run should be tailored to your school and your students. Engage a number of practitioners/older students (for example your guitar peripatetic tutor, music technology specialist, a DJ, taiko drumming specialist, a vocal coach, etc) to run short taster workshops that all students experience on a carousel basis, and then rate afterwards.	• Enables you to respond to your students' expressed activity preferences • Can accommodate large numbers of students • Provides good peer-networking opportunities for students • Allows students to interact with a wide range of practitioners, styles and genres • Enables you to signpost students to other available opportunities (for example run by your local Music Service, community music group, etc)	Music teacher or another leader who can arrange a number of taster workshops. Use of peripatetic staff, community musicians and/or older students from within the school/community. Consider working in partnership with your local Music Service or other brokering agency to plan and execute this type of project.	Workshop rooms/ spaces. Appropriate technical equipment/ instruments for hands-on sessions.	Cost is variable depending on the number of practitioners, and where the activity takes place (i.e. in the school or in an external venue).

DEVELOPING EXTRA-CURRICULAR PROVISION

Target group	Project type	Project description	Potential benefits	People	Resources	Potential cost
B	Songwriting and technology club	An after-school club that involves re-mixing and using technology to create music and videos. Use older students in the school as music technology peer-mentors, for younger students attending the club.	• Allows young people with limited musical skills or experience to participate and contribute creatively • Ideal for non-instrumentalists • Can incorporate online tutoring • Immediately gets young people making music together • Can include students of all abilities including complete beginners • Non-readers can easily join in group music-making • Facilitates peer-networking and develops group dynamics • Helps motivate students to access other activities	Either a music teacher, or one or two creative practitioners. Peer mentors.	• Access to music technology and video suite • *Writers Unblocked* materials for running a song writing club (available to download from **www.musicalfutures.org.uk/ songwriting**) Also see the Guide to Songwriting (page 101)	Creative practitioner fees (if using). Students may acquire the skills needed to continue this as a student-run club.
B	First access music club.	A music club designed specifically for previously disengaged students, giving first access to a range of rock instruments, and exploring material suggested both by the participants and the practitioners. An introduction to a variety of styles could be incorporated (e.g. blues, reggae, ska, country).	• Immediately gets young people making music together • Can include students of all abilities including complete beginners • Non-readers can easily join in group music-making • Facilitates peer-networking and develops group dynamics • Helps motivate students to access other activities	• Creative practitioners • School staff • Peer mentors	• Workshop rooms. • Range of instruments • Technical equipment • Internet access • *Breaking the Mould* materials, (available to download from **www.musicalfutures. org.uk/classroom+ workshopping**) Also see the Guide to Classroom Workshopping (page 47)	Practitioner fees (if using). In time the group may become self-programming, led by students and coordinated by peer mentors.

DEVELOPING EXTRA-CURRICULAR PROVISION

Target group	Project type	Project description	Potential benefits	People	Resources	Potential cost
C	Songwriting project	Introduction to chords, riffs, scales, lyric writing, melody, group skills and performance.	• Immediately gets young people making and creating music together • Non-readers can easily join in group music making • Extends technical, social and music skills, and builds confidence and motivation • Facilitates peer-networking and develops group dynamics • Introduces young people to a range of styles and genres	Creative practitioners.	• Workshop rooms • Range of instruments • Technical equipment • Internet access • *Writers Unblocked* materials for running a song writing club (available to download from **www.musicalfutures.org.uk/songwriting**) Also see the Guide to Songwriting (page 101)	Creative practitioners fees (if using). Students quickly acquire the skills needed to continue the pathway as a student-run club with younger students.
C	Creative ensembles	All-inclusive ensembles designed to: • Support transition from Key Stage 2 to Key Stage 3 and/or • Support students not yet ready to join a conventional ensemble Students explore a variety of improvisational techniques, collaborate to create their own pieces, and are introduced to a wide range of musical influences.	• Allows young people with limited musical skills or experience to participate in and contribute creatively to an ensemble • Non-readers can easily join in group music making • Helps to prevent 'drop-off' • Provides a good opportunity for teachers and community musicians to deliver collaboratively • Can be provided on an individual school basis or as a shared resource for a cluster of schools • Extends technical, social and musical skills and builds confidence and motivation	Preferably two creative practitioners for example one peripatetic teacher plus one school-based teacher, learning mentor or technician; older, more advanced students to act as peer-mentors	• Workshop rooms • Range of instruments • Technical equipment • *Breaking the Mould* materials, (available to download from **www.musicalfutures.org.uk/classroom+workshopping**) Also see the Guide to Classroom Workshopping (page 47)	Practitioner fees (if using)

DEVELOPING EXTRA-CURRICULAR PROVISION

Target group	Project type	Project description	Potential benefits	People	Resources	Potential cost
D	• Bands packages • Professional studio recording sessions • Showcase gig • Battle of the bands competition	Variety of activities designed by and for already engaged students, to take their music making to a new level	• Extends musical, technical and organisational skills • Builds peer networks • Provides high quality interaction with the music profession and business • Encourages independence, pro-action and initiative • Provides performance and recording experience in 'real-world' situations • Supports young people to promote their music	High quality professional performing musicians, music business professionals, recording studio engineers, venue promoters	Access to high-quality 'real-world' venues, equipment and recording studios	Variable, potential to 'earn ' income through ticket and CD sales

SECTION 3: REVIEW

The process of review is ongoing and should:

- Review projects and their operational delivery
- Allow for a joint (student/learning manager) assessment of next steps

This should involve as many of the participants in the project as possible: teacher and tutors, peer leaders and participants. You can learn as much from projects which don't go well as from those that do, so it's important from the start to create an atmosphere of constructive criticism.

It may be helpful to have a review session facilitated by someone (an older student perhaps) who was not directly involved in the project. Ensure that the positives are given as much time as the negatives, and that key learning points are noted for future projects.

Assessing student progress is a separate activity to project review, and could be undertaken termly or annually. It is a combination of Assessment for Learning and advice and guidance, both aimed at supporting the student to gain confidence in their learning to date, and identify next steps along the continuum of initial hesitation, through engagement, to confidence and independence in music learning.

CASE STUDY: HIGH STORRS SCHOOL, SHEFFIELD

After exploring Musical Futures in curriculum time, and reading the Leeds pathfinder's Personalising Extra Curricular Activities materials, James Cross – a music teacher at High Storrs School in Sheffield – explains how he adjusted their extra-curricular provision to meet the needs of all students.

" High Storrs is a large comprehensive in Sheffield. Our intake is very mixed, with around 70% of students coming from one of the most affluent areas of the city, and around 30% coming from more deprived areas.

I started to realise that while 'traditional' extra-curricular music activities were well suited to those students who had instrumental lessons (typically from the more affluent region of our intake), there wasn't really anything on offer for students who clearly had an interest in music, but who didn't play an instrument.

I decided to set up a music technology club, which took into account the personalised, informal approach of Musical Futures. It wasn't just a case of thinking of an activity that the target students may like and running it – the club was designed from the outset to be personalised to their needs. I gave very careful thought to how often it would run, how it would run, how it would be organised, and what kind of 'feel' it would have. The word 'club' was out. The phrase 'you decide' was the focus.

The resulting activity was 'My Sound'. Students were invited to 'take their music in their own direction', using technology. Everything about the activity was flexible – students were made aware of the possibilities, and they approached me with their needs and ideas. While some students

DEVELOPING EXTRA-CURRICULAR PROVISION

wanted to use Reason to make beats, others wanted to use the studio to record vocals.

Students would come to me armed with ideas for backings, lyrics scribbled on the back of worksheets from other subjects, and enthusiastic pleas for as much studio time as possible. Students who had long lists of behaviour incidents and exclusions were choosing to stay after school to make music. Students who struggled in English lessons were spending hours of their own time writing lyrics. Students of all ages who never would have dreamed of taking part in extra-curricular music were thriving. One even begged 'Sir, please phone my mum and tell her I've got a detention', as he was worried that his mother would never believe he had stayed in school by choice, and would assume he was up to something that he shouldn't be!

As a result of the activity, I'm now exploring personalising our Key Stage 4 courses, by running a more accessible alternative to GCSE music. I'm also consulting with English staff to design a literacy project, building on the willingness of these students to write lyrics at home. During many Key Stage 3 Musical Futures lessons, 6th-form music technology students record groups of MCs in the studio. In the same way that guitars make the Musical Futures experience more credible to some students, working in the studio with a professional vocal microphone makes it more authentic to others.

The only problem I encountered is that there simply aren't enough hours in the school week to accommodate all the groups of students who want studio time. It's taken over my lunchtimes and any spare time I have after school, which can be difficult around exam season. But, however busy I am, each time I'm approached by a student in the corridor, I find it impossible to say no.

So, if your school has a mixed intake like ours, take a step back and consider how you might be able to personalise your extra-curricular activities to appeal to students who may be overlooked at the moment. For me, working with these students is by far the most rewarding aspect of the job. **"**

High Storrs School is a Musical Futures Champion School

Equipment and Music Technology

A music department with limited resources **should not** feel that Musical Futures isn't for them. Musical Futures first and foremost is a pedagogical approach, and many of the ideas presented here can be implemented using instruments and resources that should be available in most school music departments.

It is clear, however, that where schools have been able to source equipment and technology that has credibility among students, it can have a positive impact on their motivation for and enjoyment of music making and learning.

Equipment

Musical Futures approaches are centred around practical music making, therefore inevitably require instruments to be available. The following illustrates equipment/instruments that are typically used in Musical Futures:

Instrument	How/when it gets used
Equipment to play audio through – for example CD players, MP3 players, iPods, computers	The majority of Musical Futures projects involve listening, either through students working in small groups, or as a whole group with some sort of backing track, therefore audio equipment is essential in most lessons.
A selection of guitars (acoustic and electric), bass guitars, and associated leads and amps	Guitars/bass guitars tend to feature heavily in Musical Futures. Electric guitars hold particular appeal due to their association with rock and popular music, however acoustic guitars can be equally popular. It is unrealistic to expect a school to have enough guitars for every student, however having a number of guitars available can enhance motivation.
Keyboards	Keyboards are usually already available in music departments, and are very versatile for use in Musical Futures work, for example as a drum machine/rhythm section, to choose different timbres to replicate sounds, and for melodic and harmonic parts. If keyboards are being used with instruments such as drum kits and electric guitars, they will require an amplifier.
Drum kit/drum pads	Most music departments have at least one drum kit, which if necessary can be rotated among students to use. Alternatively, you can split drum kits up so that one group has a bass-drum, tom and crash cymbal, and another group has a floor-tom, snare and ride cymbal for example. Even two drums, or one drum and one cymbal in a group can make a big difference. Electronic drum kits have proved popular among students, as have electronic drum pads – and these options both have the added benefits of being easier to store, and having volume control.
Microphones	It is useful to have a stock of good quality vocal microphones available, for students using their voices through singing, rapping, MCing, etc.
Violins	Violins have often been used in Musical Futures projects. Image Junction (page 116) suggests a way of using violins as an instrumental group, and the Band Instrumental Work project (page 88) has also made use of violins as a carousel option.
Percussion	Tuned and un-tuned percussion is frequently used, especially if drum kits are not available.
Other melodic and harmonic instruments	In Musical Futures projects, when instruments are made available to students, they often will experiment and find ways of integrating them. Therefore no instrument should be disregarded with this approach.

If your department is able to invest in some additional equipment, our recommendation would be that you buy good quality equipment – even if it means buying less – rather than purchasing lots of poorer quality gear. Equipment in Musical Futures will be used frequently and heavily, therefore poorer quality equipment is unlikely to be such a good investment.

TECHNICAL SUPPORT

If you can organise some technician support in your music department, it can greatly improve the maintenance of the equipment, and also saves you valuable time. Where Musical Futures schools have been able to secure technical support it has ranged from:

- An appointed music technician, who oversees all equipment, storage and music technology in the music department

- A peripatetic teacher with good technical knowledge, who is employed for some extra time to maintain guitars, amps, etc

- An older student in the school who has some technical knowledge and either volunteers or is employed to maintain guitars, amps, etc

Many schools have found innovative ways of increasing the equipment in their music department, often in consultation and collaboration with students, who can take a real ownership over this process. Consider some of the following:

- Put on a fundraiser concert/gig of Musical Futures work (battle of the bands, Musical Futures showcase, etc) with the proceeds going towards equipment

- Ask students to bring in their own instruments from home

- Run an instrument amnesty among parents/carers to ask for unwanted instruments to be donated to the music department

- Source unwanted audio equipment from other school departments (for example PE, languages)

- Ask students to write a fundraising bid for the headteacher's consideration

HEALTH AND SAFETY

It is important that teachers and students are fully aware of the health and safety implications of working with electrical equipment in the classroom. Many teachers give demonstration lessons throughout Musical Futures (especially at the beginning of projects) about plugging guitars into amps, not having trailing leads, etc, and we would thoroughly recommend this. Noise levels need to be monitored to ensure that students aren't damaging their hearing by having equipment turned up too loudly, and drummers should wear ear-plugs.

NOTE

www.soundadvice.info/ provides information on noise levels in schools and colleges, with some practical advice for minimising risk.

www.musiciansunion.org.uk/site/cms/ contentviewarticle.asp?article=484 provides information on a range of health and safety issues in schools and colleges.

EQUIPMENT AND MUSIC TECHNOLOGY

MUSICAL FUTURES AND ROLAND

Siôn Kemp, Education Business Development Manager at Roland UK (**www.roland.co.uk**) gives some advice on equipping your music department

Why should a department invest in good quality equipment for Musical Futures?

Our experience shows that if you buy cheap, you buy twice. Consider investing in equipment that has been built for heavy use, that has excellent quality of sound, and where the 'feel' of the instrument is great. These factors are important in motivating students to use and respect the equipment.

If a department could invest in some equipment, what would you recommend?

Electronic drum kits can give great results in teaching and learning environments – students can plug-in headphones as well as turn them down. Students can also play along with music from their iPods, and they are compatible with MIDI, PCs and Macs. Electronic drum pads (such as the Handsonic range) give students a tactile experience as you play them with your hands, and are also compatible with MIDI. Also consider equipment that enables you to record and loop performances on the fly, as these can be good ways of exploring composition and improvisation.

What is your advice for maintaining equipment?

With equipment that gets used heavily, consider:

- Using a small amount of super-glue to stick volume knobs and faders down so they can't be removed and go missing; the same thing also works well with products that have washers around the jack input – avoiding losing the jack socket inside the product. This also applies to the jack output of guitars and basses

- If your headphones use adapters that can be removed/unscrewed, then a tiny drop of superglue will stop them going missing. (Make sure you won't want to use the headphones on equipment that has a small headphone jack)

- A small multi-tool is always handy with screw drivers/Alan keys/hex keys; it doesn't need to have a blade/knife

- Make sure any thumb screws and head tuning lugs on drums are done up tightly

- Guitars/basses should be put on stands or wall hangers

- Dust covers generally keep the condition of the instruments in good shape

- Re-useable Velcro cable ties attach to one end of a jack cable and keep it tangle free while storing coiled-up (saving hours of untangling time), as well as being useful behind studio gear keeping that 'spaghetti junction' in check

- 'Cable labels' are also very handy (or marker cable ties) so you know which cable is plugged into which socket or output. This is particularly handy when you have many cables being used together. Even just simple colour coding helps

- Plastic tipped drum sticks are less likely to cause damage to an electronic mesh head drum (as wooden tips can splinter and cause perforations)

- Consider investing in rechargeable batteries and a charger if using electronic equipment that requires batteries. They're more cost effective and kinder on the environment

- Knowing how to do a factory reset on electronic equipment is useful if a student has altered settings and you need to get it back to how it was. Often this is easily found by typing in Google: factory reset/name of product

- When it comes to cleaning the equipment Servisol antistatic foam cleanser is good, and is suitable for plastic, metal and most other materials. (Make sure products are not plugged in if electrical; and test on a small area if using on a lacquered, polished or laminated surface.) Micro-fibre cleaning cloths are also best as they don't leave bits of fluff/ material behind

Do you have any advice for storing equipment?

If space is at a premium, consider exploring smaller pieces of equipment that do a similar job. For example, instead of a drum kit, consider an electronic drum pad (for example the Handsonic) with hi-hat and kick pedal, which would take up half of the space. Electronic drums can easily be folded away for storage. Any smaller items that cannot be secured should either be in a room that is lockable or be kept in a secure cabinet.

Music Technology

Technology plays a crucial role in the lives of young people, with many making music on computers, online, using recording equipment to upload, remix, publish work, share music, listen to music, compose, perform, review and more. Therefore we recommend that technology that is meaningful and relevant to students is integrated into all Musical Futures projects.

Our top ten general tips for integrating technology into Musical Futures are:

1. **The Internet** – for students to source tracks they might intend to learn or to use to guide composition. Students can download lyrics, chords and source guitar/bass/drum tab, etc

2. **NUMU (www.numu.org.uk)** – free website for tracking progress, allowing students to share work and get feedback. Also valuable for teachers to store recordings for assessment and to pass on comments and feedback

3. **Audacity** – free recording and audio editing software. Invaluable tool for capturing recordings on computers. Audio tracks can be edited and exported in wav and MP3 format ready for upload to NUMU or to a phone, MP3 player, etc

4. **Sequencing/recording software** – although many students are enthusiastic about getting their hands on guitars, drums and other instruments there will always be some (often those interested

EQUIPMENT AND MUSIC TECHNOLOGY

primarily in urban music) that will be more inspired by creating beats and backing tracks using computer-based sequencers. The simpler programmes are usually the best unless students already have a background in music software. Current budget favourites are **M-Audio Session** and **Cakewalk Music Creator 4** (for Windows PC users) and **Garageband** (only for Apple Mac users). Many schools already use **Steinberg's Cubase** and **Logic** (although more expensive) available for either Windows PC or Apple Mac users. They also have guitar and bass guitar tuners. Students can create their own beats using sequencers which is useful for bands without a drummer or for those who want a more programmed/loop-based sound. This can of course extend to adding bass lines, harmony parts, etc, and using the software to record their experiments and capture new ideas

5. **Sequencers in performance** – any of the programs mentioned above can also be used as a live performance tool. Students can use them to play virtual instruments and to create backing textures

6. **MP3 recorders** – available in budget and pro specifications, an excellent alternative to using computers for recording and more easily portable

7. **Electronic drums** – have several advantages over acoustic drums, firstly that you can control the volume which makes it easier to balance the kit with other instruments. Secondly they take up less room than an acoustic kit. They come in various types from small pad-based units to full drum kit style kits

8. **Technology support** – it is one thing to have the equipment, quite another to stay on top of maintenance and problem solving. Some investment in support from technician staff and/or from trusted students can support the smooth running of Musical Futures

9. **Mobile phones** – depending on individual school policies, these can be very useful. Students can listen to tracks on their phone, can usually record audio with them and capture video clips. This can be useful to help them remember how specific parts are played. They also *always* have them with them, so are unlikely to lose recordings

10. **Your students** – technology is ever changing, and students are often the first to experiment with emerging technologies. It is difficult to stay on top of all the latest developments, trusted music outlets can be helpful for keeping abreast as can a subscription to a music technology based magazine or website (for example Sound On Sound magazine and website) so use your students as a resource – through peer-to-peer coaching and keeping you informed – wherever possible

In some cases, it may be appropriate to use your schools' generic ICT suite for music technology work. This can have the advantage of enabling links between music and other curricular areas, and it also shows students how music learning can be accessed outside of the music department.

Electrifying Music by David Ashworth, was commissioned by Musical Futures and is a study of integrating ICT into music education. It discusses ways in which music teachers can gain valuable support and networking with music technology, considers some of the practical issues of embedding ICT into the curriculum, considers ways of linking in- and out-of-school ICT experiences, and considers the potential for using computer-generated music alongside conventional instruments. Download the pamphlet from **www.musicalfutures.org.uk/electifying+music**. Some of the approaches to working with technology outlined in the pamphlet are now being presented in more detail on **www.teachingmusic.org.uk** (notably videoclips and how to guides).

Also, the *Creative Guide to Music Technology* by Richard Sabey (first published as part of the Leeds Musical Futures pathfinder project) takes teachers unsure of music technology through the basic processes of recording, sampling, sequencing, looping, MIDI, mixing and more. Download the guide from **www.musicalfutures.org.uk/equipment+and +technology**.

NUMU

NUMU (**www.numu.org.uk**) is a free online tool that has been developed through Musical Futures. It is a space for students to publish their work, compete in charts, develop customised web pages and connect with others safely. It has been designed to fully engage students, while at the same time provides flexible tools for teachers to support students learning in a range of settings. For many schools, NUMU is a critical part of their Musical Futures delivery. It completes the process of rehearsal and performance, as it enables students to learn how to record, process, mix and publish their own work.

Signing up to NUMU will give you a school-based record label, where your students can create their own accounts, listen to other's music, upload their own music, and add blogs and videos to their pages. As a teacher/practitioner, you have full control over this process – you check and activate student accounts, approve your students work, and monitor for any inappropriate content. You can also use NUMU to create online projects to support Musical Futures activities.

Only schools and education establishments can join, meaning that while the public can listen to the music on the site, no personal information or pictures are visible.

NUMU can support Musical Futures work by:

- Enabling students to create their own musical identity through a personalised homepage
- Enabling students to listen to their own performances and compositions
- Using blogs for students to reflect on their musical progress
- Complete homework online
- Access and download sound files and resources to enable students to rehearse outside the classroom.

EQUIPMENT AND MUSIC TECHNOLOGY

SIGNING UP TO NUMU

You don't have to be 'doing' Musical Futures to be able to sign up to NUMU – it is free for anybody to join.

Teachers

- Go to **www.numu.org.uk** and click on 'join'

- Once your school has been approved, your school record label will be **www.numu.org.uk/yourschool**

- You can add a label logo by clicking the edit icon underneath the name of your label in the 'Website' section. Click 'Browse' to locate the picture on your computer, and then 'Upload'

- To approve a student account before it goes live, click on 'Artists/ Writers', where all new artists will be listed. Click 'Approve All' to activate all accounts, or individually select the ones you want to approve and click 'Save'

- To check and approve work, go to the 'New Content' section, and click on individual students' names. You can then add, edit or delete anything on their page. If you approve the work click 'Go Live'. The new content will then be visible to the public

- To suspend or trust a student, go to the 'Artists' section, and check the suspend or trust box next to their name and click 'Save'. Suspended artists cannot log into the site at all, but their page is still visible. Trusted students do not to have their work approved by a publisher before it goes live

- Create a project, which is a teacher-created page where you can upload music, images, text and other files. Music added to projects is not included in the charts – therefore you can upload commercial music to use as examples. Only your students can download resources from your projects

Students

- Direct students to **www.numu.org.uk/join/yourschool**

- Personalise their page by clicking 'Add a picture' in the Gallery box, browse to locate picture and click 'upload'

- Blog by clicking 'Add' in the Blog box, and entering text

CASE STUDY: SHEFFIELD PARK ACADEMY

Head of Music, Jenny Farn, was keen to develop the music curriculum and tailor it to the specific needs of her students through exploring NUMU as a tool to engage students, tackle poor self-esteem and confidence, as well as develop a broader music curriculum where students are encouraged to take part in performances and personalised learning is supported.

❝ In the past, there had been large numbers of students who were uncomfortable about actively participating in performances and who had been unused to doing anything as part of a whole class. Generally, confidence in their ability to perform as well as their self-esteem had been low. NUMU has been an invaluable tool in helping to raise self-esteem by giving status to their work. Confidence in using ICT has increased and there are now opportunities for students' music to be opened up to a

EQUIPMENT AND MUSIC TECHNOLOGY

whole new audience including friends, family and the community. In addition, a real enthusiasm for completing performance and composition tasks and then recording them has been generated, leading to a more independent or personalised learning experience. Regular showcasing of music via the website has offered opportunities for students to demonstrate their potential to achieve and has fostered a real sense of self worth.

All students at the school have an online account. They are encouraged to check the number of 'listens' to the tracks they upload in a bid to motivate them to produce good work. They are further motivated by the comments left by their peers and by staff. By using the site to listen to and review music written by their peers both in and out of school, locally and nationally, they have developed an awareness of different types of music and now strive to attain similar or higher standards. In terms of teaching and learning, the students are encouraged to be more responsible for their work. Performance and composition tasks are recorded and uploaded to the site by the students themselves.

NUMU features in music lessons on a fortnightly basis, is used in homework assignments, and forms the basis for an after-school club. Additional adults have been recruited to support learning and include a music technician (currently the guitar and drum teacher) and volunteers from the community. Approaches to teaching and learning have inevitably changed due to the more practical and performance orientated route that the Sheffield Park music curriculum is taking. Staff have undergone a personal programme of development by learning the drums and they are planning to take their Grade 1 Rock School guitar!

During Business and Enterprise week at the Academy, links were drawn by discussing and researching musicians such as Radiohead who use the Internet to launch their music and the implications of this. NUMU has also been used as part of the Academy's Gifted and Talented programme and to forge links with feeder primary schools by having a local NUMU network.

Although this work is still in its infancy, its impact can be evidenced through the increased enjoyment, engagement and motivation of the students. One Year 9 group complained that they couldn't use NUMU in the ICT rooms because it had been blocked by school.

Competing in the NUMU chart and having a global audience has really encouraged students to work together and produce music for others to listen to. A particular recording of a Year 7 call and response performance had received over 50 'listens' including the vast majority of the Year 7 class who performed it.

NUMU has already had an impact on less confident students who now feel that they have a real role to play in music making. 〝

www.numu.org.uk/spark

Buildings, Space and Musical Futures

Having the right sort of space available is a major consideration when implementing Musical Futures. It is not just about having lots of break-out spaces for students to work in, but also about ensuring that the overall environment and atmosphere of the music department is one in which students are able to be creative.

THE REALITY

Music facilities vary greatly from school to school. In the least ideal situations there is one classroom, often surrounded by classes teaching other subjects. In schools with more space, practice rooms are often occupied by instrumental staff teaching individuals or small groups of students.

In reality many music teachers are working in inadequate facilities, and lack of space was one of the major obstacles quoted by teachers feeling unable to take on Musical Futures in the Institute of Education survey.

However, dynamic music lessons often take place in far-from-ideal conditions. Good music teachers will find ways of making Musical Futures work within whatever space they have available. They have adapted a range of strategies, some of which we list below. If you find yourself with limited space, we suggest:

- Initially try Musical Futures with one class of students, if necessary having groups of students in corridors, canteen, hall, etc. If you start to see results in terms of student motivation, attitude, enjoyment and attainment, collect data and student feedback so that you can lobby your senior management for more appropriate space to be made available

- Avoid running two Musical Futures classes at the same time, as this considerably limits the space and equipment available and can prove frustrating for teachers and students. If two classes are timetabled together, consider having one following a classroom-based project (particularly if you have a designated keyboard or computer room available), while the other follows Musical Futures, and then swap the classes over. Again, if you start to see positive results, student feedback can help to ensure timetabling is done more sensitively towards the music department

- Avoid two groups of students sharing a space, as this can lead to frustration and distraction on behalf of the students. If this is unavoidable, consider investing in equipment where multiple headphones can be used

- Consider rotating students around the spaces on a weekly basis so they feel they have a fair 'go' in the better practice rooms

- Negotiate with instrumental staff to organise their hours around busy curriculum times. If there is a possibility for an instrumental teacher to be paid to support a Musical Futures lesson, then this can free up space and give staff an idea of what goes on in the classroom

- Be open with students about the restrictions. If they are enthusiastic about Musical Futures and they understand the principles behind it then they are likely to be prepared to share equipment and space

- If there are particular hotspots during the week where noise pollution may be an issue, make students aware of this and negotiate some rules about keeping sound to a minimum. If they are working outside the music room, encourage them to understand that if the noise levels are too high, it is likely that they will not be allowed to use that space in future lessons. Make staff teaching around the department aware that there may be noise and assure them that you will do your best to keep disruption to a minimum

Alcester High School in Warwickshire (a Musical Futures Champion School) has three practice spaces and a main classroom and, with large classes, this is not generally enough space for Musical Futures. The Head of Music has therefore established a rotation system every lesson, whereby half of the groups go into practice spaces and do Musical Futures work, while the other groups do a whole class activity in the classroom, such as a listening or music technology task, that directly relates to their practical work. Halfway through the lesson, the groups swap over. This means that every group gets the opportunity to do practical work, and because they have a shorter period of time (30 minutes) they generally are on task and get on with their work. To help facilitate this, the Head of Music has been able to secure a professional musician who supports the groups with their practical work while the Head of Music oversees the listening/music technology work.

THE IDEAL

Based upon feedback from schools following Musical Futures, the ideal set-up for Musical Futures work would be:

- Separate breakout spaces (between three and six rooms for each classroom) equipped with piano/keyboard, sound system, networked computer and enough electrical sockets for equipment

- Up to four instrumental teaching spaces with piano, sound system and networked computer in each

- Technology in every practice space (one networked computer minimum)

- Recording studio

- Full sound proofing

BUILDINGS, SPACE AND MUSICAL FUTURES

- Informal space or a staff room/kitchen for instrumental and classroom teachers and students to network, with notice board to aid communication, and a networked computer and printer to prepare lesson materials
- Admin office with networked computer
- Performance space
- Separate storage for (a) electrical equipment and (b) student's instruments
- A central information point for students

Ideally, these spaces should be located close enough together for teachers to circulate among groups of students with ease, yet far enough away from other subject areas to avoid complaints.

BUILDING SCHOOLS FOR THE FUTURE

Building Schools for the Future (BSF) is a Government programme to transform secondary education in England. Ian Sutton, from BSF, explores some concepts for a music learning space.

In January 2009, a group of music practitioners from the education, community and professional sectors met at Morpeth School in Tower Hamlets to consider what music spaces being developed through Building Schools for the Future programme should look like, especially if they are incorporating approaches such as Musical Futures. The following is an outcome of these discussions, and represents a series of ideas and concepts that you could discuss in your school.

Key considerations for designing a space include:

- A music space needs to reflect the changing use of schools in general, with a growing emphasis on extended services, co-location of services and community use. Therefore, the design of music spaces needs to consider how it can respond to the needs of the community and the way people engage with music at a local level. If there is a lack of affordable rehearsal space or recording studios in the area, can the school provide these facilities?
- Spaces need to be a combination of 'flexible' and 'fixed' (see page 197)
- Adequate storage space is critical and should be positioned in such a way that teachers and learners can easily access what they need close to the space in which they are working. Storage also needs to be organised in such a way that instruments and equipment can be quickly and methodically packed up and returned to storage at the end of the session
- Sound proofing is essential. Some teachers/practitioners felt that current regulations relating to the acoustic requirements in school spaces were inadequate for modern music making and needed to be revised. Morpeth School (see the Case Study on page 123) had been able to take advantage of the natural sound-proofing offered by adapting basement rooms as rehearsal spaces and hoped to recreate this feature in a new build. Any new build should be positioned so that sound is projected away from neighbouring buildings, including nearby housing. We would advise you to consult your architect or ask

BUILDINGS, SPACE AND MUSICAL FUTURES

an acoustic design consultant to prepare a design specification for your individual requirements

- Heating and ventilation should not be secondary considerations, as heating and ventilation systems can be noisy, damaging to sensitive equipment, and unhealthy for students – especially in an environment in which acoustic considerations can result in windowless, enclosed spaces. Similarly, lack of natural light can be detrimental to performance, mood and ambience. Advances in technology make the use of glass in sound-proofed situations much more of a reality

- Recording and playback facilities in every room. By using hand-held 'field recorders' and other portable devices, or by linking each room to a central recording studio teachers/practitioners and students would be able to utilise instant playback as part of their music learning progression

- Access and Circulation. Doors need be wide enough and easy to open when you're carrying for example a double bass or a guitar amp. Also, positioning your main entrance so that it's accessible from the street makes it easier to use the space beyond the school day (thereby increasing access for students who may want to rehearse in their own time, or to promote access by the community). Making sure you have the right number of doors (properly labelled) is essential for public licensing. Personal safety, security and behaviour – whether related to students or visitors – are important issues. Clear lines of visibility including liberal use of window space and wide corridors will allow monitoring of activity and ease of access

The following outlines a concept for how a music department might be structured into four 'Zones', and how they might be used:

Zone 1: Flexible	A music department's list of music activities can be extensive and varied, with greatly differing spatial requirements. Therefore 'flexibility' is the constant refrain in any discussion about space. The conceptual solution would be a single, large room intersected by a network of soundproof retractable walls that could be worked into any arrangement of smaller rooms at any time. A more practical option would be a room large enough for group instruction with a series of four or five smaller 'break out' rooms leading from it. Also, there is no particular need for any of these rooms to be square. A circle or oval space could work better in terms of students being able to face each other or focus on a group leader.
Zone 2: Fixed	Despite a general call for flexibility, some spaces still need to remain 'fixed': a recording studio and space for the workforce (including rest space and administration space) for example. This 'Fixed' zone may be best placed at the core of the space so that its functions can radiate into each of the 'Flexible' spaces leading from it.
Zone 3: Social	A music space in a school should not be a sanitised arts centre but a space that is designed by and for students. Having social spaces such as a seating area, informal performing area, possibly even a café, gives students a space in which they can interact. A public space of this kind could also provide opportunities to generate income by promoting community use of the space.
Zone 4: Storage	It is impossible to over-emphasise the importance of storage. In the model below, storage is designed in such a way as to be held centrally, like a carousel, and therefore accessible from any room with minimum effort. Failing this, making sure as many boxes, flight cases or pieces of equipment as possible are on wheels would be critical.

BUILDINGS, SPACE AND MUSICAL FUTURES

The following represents a conceptual idea of what a music space could look like:

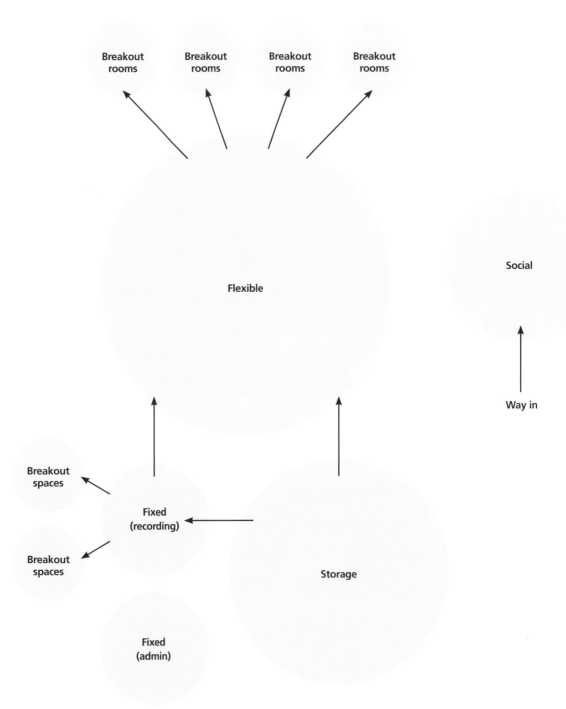

CASE STUDY: SIMON BALLE SCHOOL

This case study provides one example of how a school has re-worked its resources to create a building fit-for-purpose.

Simon Balle School is a mixed comprehensive specialist humanities school in Hertfordshire. The school participated in the second pilot year of the Musical Futures Hertfordshire pathfinder work on informal learning. Over the past two years the existing music department building has been extended, staffed and resourced to create a new, innovative music department.

THE BUILDING

Simon Balle's music department takes into account the broad range of opportunities students wanted, both in Musical Futures and other work. Practice spaces are therefore divided into instrumental teaching areas and curriculum areas. This means that no Musical Futures lessons (or other music lessons) are lacking in space due to instrumental teachers occupying rooms, and instrumental teaching staff can have full timetables without the disruption of Musical Futures lessons.

The building is on two levels, and is split into curriculum areas (ground floor) and instrumental teaching areas (first floor). All equipment is permanently stored in the rooms, meaning that Musical Futures lessons can start with little set-up time.

BUILDINGS, SPACE AND MUSICAL FUTURES

Room	Resources
Classroom 1	<ul><li>14 IMac computers with Midi keyboards</li><li>PA system</li><li>Mixing desk</li><li>Piano</li><li>Drum kit</li><li>Electric guitar, bass guitar and amps</li></ul>
Classroom 2	<ul><li>14 IMac computers with Midi keyboards</li><li>PA system</li><li>Mixing desk</li><li>Piano</li><li>Drum kit</li><li>Electric guitar, bass guitar and amps</li></ul>
Curriculum Practice Room	<ul><li>Electric drum kit</li><li>Electric guitar, bass guitar and amps</li><li>IMac computer with MIDI keyboard</li></ul>
Curriculum Practice Room 2	<ul><li>Electric drum kit</li><li>Electric guitar, bass guitar and amps</li><li>IMac computer with MIDI keyboard</li></ul>
Curriculum Practice Room 3	<ul><li>Electric drum kit</li><li>Electric guitar, bass guitar and amps</li><li>IMac computer with MIDI keyboard</li></ul>
Curriculum Practice Room 4	<ul><li>Electric drum kit</li><li>Electric guitar, bass guitar and amps</li><li>IMac computer with MIDI keyboard</li><li>Acoustic piano</li></ul>
Curriculum Practice Room 5	<ul><li>Electric drum kit</li><li>Electric guitar, bass guitar and amps</li><li>IMac computer with MIDI keyboard</li><li>Electric piano</li></ul>
Percussion studio	<ul><li>Two acoustic drum kits</li><li>Store for all percussion (djembes, samba equipment)</li></ul>

Room	Resources
Rehearsal room	• Grand piano • PA system • All music stands
Recording studio	Live room: • Drum kit • Electric guitar, bass guitar and amps Control room: • Mackie 24-8 mixing desk • G5 Mac pro (networked) • Motu firewire interface – 8 in 8 out
Instrumental teaching practice room 1	• Piano • PA • Filing cabinet
Instrumental teaching practice room 2	• Piano • PA • Filing cabinet
Instrumental teaching practice room 3	• Piano • PA • Filing cabinet
Instrumental teaching practice room 4	• Piano • PA • Filing cabinet
Instrumental teaching practice room 5	• Piano • PA • Filing cabinet

TECHNOLOGY

Technology is fully integrated and embedded into everything that the department does, which is facilitated through the Mac computers which are throughout the department. All computers in the building are networked, meaning that a student can do a recording in the studio, save their work into the networked area, and do a mix of their work using any of the other computers in the building. All student work is uploaded onto NUMU (**www.numu.org.uk**).

SECTION 4: ORGANISATION AND DESIGN

BUILDINGS, SPACE AND MUSICAL FUTURES

USAGE

The department now has the space and facilities to run practical, Musical Futures style activity throughout Years 8 and Year 9 for all students. It has fixed equipment in every room, and technician support to ensure that instruments are regularly maintained.

The facilities are in constant use through the following:

- Curriculum time, used for Musical Futures and MF style activity
- Students can book into a room through a booking system run by reception – rooms get booked up from 8.15am
- Music technology students use the facilities in the evening for their work
- Out-of-hours Rockschool and urban music workshops
- Rehearsals after school every night
- A community theatre group runs a session once a week until 9pm
- Base for the Hertfordshire Music Service hub – uses for Saturday morning and evening instrumental teaching, and wind band rehearsals
- All instrumental teaching practice rooms are in constant use for instrumental teaching throughout the day and evening

IMPACT

The knock-on effect on students has been that Musical Futures has been made even more successful, as all students in Years 8 and 9 are able to participate (compared to before the new build when classes had to either rotate, or couldn't do Musical Futures). The new department has raised the profile of music among students, particularly those who didn't have much interest in music beforehand. The technology threaded through the department means that they have much more success in appealing to students who have an interest in urban music.

Music department staff provide ongoing CPD to other staff members on technology, and all instrumental teaching staff are given access to a laptop with Freeware programme Audacity pre-loaded, so that they can capture recordings of their students during instrumental lessons.

The music department is used not just by the school and the Music Service, but by the wider community as well. The teachers have dedicated time for outreach work to local primary schools, which can involve classes from feeder primaries visiting the music department for sessions on Garageband, or vocal workshops hosted at the school.

NOTE

A more detailed version of this case study is available to download from www. musicalfutures.org.uk/music+depart ment+of+the+future, also see http:// simonballe.virtualschools.net/

Musical Futures and External Observers: Advice for Dealing with Senior Managers and Inspectors

For many music teachers/practitioners, Musical Futures can be a departure from the norm, a leap of faith, and a step outside their comfort zone. In the survey on Musical Futures carried out by the Institute of Education (available on **www.musicalfutures.org.uk/c/reports+and+articles**), only 21% of teachers indicated that they received support from senior management to run Musical Futures, with the majority stating that they either received no support at all, or that there was little awareness of Musical Futures among their senior leaders.

While many music teachers/practitioners take on Musical Futures in relative isolation, with little or no support from within the school, it is much more effective and sustainable in the long-term if there is whole-school buy-in for Musical Futures. But unless handled carefully, the very people you need to have behind you might consider it too risky and disruptive an innovation. This section therefore offers some advice on what to consider when presenting Musical Futures to others.

The first likely challenge you'll face will be advocating Musical Futures as an important strategic development for your school and far more than your students simply 'having fun'. The programme has gained attention, nationally and internationally, because of its contribution to finding innovative ways to engage learners – not just music learners. Many of our pathfinder headteachers unanimously told us that Musical Futures had impacted across the whole school, and that its approaches were applicable to many curriculum areas. This led to a further Paul Hamlyn Foundation initiative, Learning Futures, which will be testing out this wider applicability during 2009–11.

NOTE

The initial pamphlet *Learning Futures: Next Practice in Learning and Teaching* (available from **www.phf.org.uk/landing. asp?id=368**) outlines the pedagogic theory and principles which originated in Musical Futures and sets them within a whole school improvement context. Both Musical Futures and Learning Futures are part of a bigger shift to more progressive strategies for student engagement, alongside initiatives such as the RSA's 'Opening Minds' curriculum, 'Studio Schools', Learning to Learn and a freeing-up of the Key Stage 3 curriculum.

SECTION 4: ORGANISATION AND DESIGN

MUSICAL FUTURES AND EXTERNAL OBSERVERS

The Musical Futures website (**www.musicalfutures.org.uk/testimonies**) has a series of video interviews on Musical Futures' wider significance, one of which describes it as 'the most advanced form of personalisation within any curricular area'. The pamphlet *Personalising Music Learning* (available to download from **www.musicalfutures.org.uk/c/pamphlets**) explains how this is made real and, with schools eager to make their curriculum (especially at Key Stage 3) more appealing, engaging and personalised. These arguments can be useful in highlighting the cutting-edge nature of the programme and why your senior management should be considering it. Still further testimonials and evidence of the impact of Musical Futures can be found in the pamphlet *From Vision to Practice: Summary of Key Findings* (also available from the Musical Futures website).

Assuming you now have the go-ahead from your headteacher, you would be well-advised to brief your senior managers and teaching colleagues on its likely impact – not all will see a vibrant and loud music block as a good thing!

Initially, you may want to:

- Ask your Local Authority music adviser/Music Service head to accompany you to staff meetings to stress the importance of the pedagogical approach advocated by Musical Futures

- Ensure senior managers understand the philosophy and strong pedagogical grounding of Musical Futures

- Invite a member of the senior management team to a Musical Futures lesson, highlighting any students that are working particularly well – especially if those students do not necessarily have a good track-record in other subjects

- Build up video and audio evidence of student work to demonstrate progress and attainment

- Have a Musical Futures group perform in an assembly or school concert – particularly students who haven't performed or participated before

- Run a practical workshop or do a presentation at a whole-school INSET session to ensure that other staff members are aware of what is happening in the music department

It is worth highlighting to senior managers that lessons are likely to be co-constructed (content and curriculum created by you *and* your students) and will evidence:

- Student engagement: high levels of motivation, excitement, and usually of noise

- Independent learning: students working, often unsupervised, in small groups, on instruments of their choice, setting their own objectives and deciding their learning pathways

- Meta-cognition and Learning to Learn: students discovering their preferred learning styles and developing their own identity as a musical learner

- Practical learning: workshop-style sessions with all students playing instruments; lessons take on the pattern of 'real-world' rehearsals

- Extended and accelerated learning: students often continue with work in their own time – practising, downloading material for the next lesson, discussing their work, listening to their recordings for the next lesson.

○ Peer learning: students leading others in learning activities

○ Three-part lessons can still be present – with a starter, main activity and plenary

OFSTED

Visiting observers often comment that there is an obvious and immediate contrast between a typical Musical Futures session and more didactic, transmissive teaching. Students are clearly animated, on-task, and enjoying their learning. The follow-up comment usually highlights an anxiety shared by many heads of music and senior managers: 'but what will OFSTED (the schools inspection agency) make of it?!'

During the pathfinder phase of Musical Futures, it was fair to say that these concerns were legitimate. With OFSTED's historical emphasis upon the teacher's role, there were fears that the teacher would be seen to have made themselves redundant, and there would not be much of what would typically be thought of as 'teaching' taking place. However, with the shift in OFSTED's focus, to the quality of *learning* taking place (and a recognition that learning is usually more effective when teacher support is requested rather than 'delivered') Musical Futures seems less radical.

In theory, observations of Musical Futures lessons, either by Ofsted or by a Senior Management/Local Authority staff member, should be no different in terms of preparation and execution than a 'normal' music lesson. Inspectors generally seem impressed by the learning that takes place in Musical Futures, and by the often excellent examples of engaging students in relevant musical provision, increasing their musical understanding, evidence of motivation, enjoyment and attitude towards music lessons, and by the musical progression implicit in Musical Futures work.

However, it is advisable to give inspectors a full briefing on what to look out for (especially non-subject specialists) before observing Musical Futures lessons.

The following are some key elements that Ofsted has identified in the recent report 'Making More of Music' as being good or outstanding practice. We would expect any school 'doing' Musical Futures in the way that it is intended to be able to show clear evidence of all of the below:

○ Teaching should have a clear musical learning focus, and there should be depth and quality to the music learning taking place

○ There should be an emphasis on musical quality, and students should be clear on how to improve their work

○ Practical music-making activity should be at the heart of all work

○ Links should be made between students' own musical experiences and those the school provides so that students' own interests can be developed

○ Teachers should demonstrate and model to their students, showing their own expertise and clearly demonstrating what is expected of the

FURTHER READING

The Ofsted website (**www.ofsted. gov.uk**) contains the 2009 report on music education *Making More of Music*, which makes reference to Musical Futures. During the pathfinder years of Musical Futures, the Paul Hamlyn Foundation commissioned Ofsted to carry out an evaluation of Musical Futures work in a sample of schools. This evaluation is also available from the Ofsted website, by searching for 'Musical Futures'.

NOTE

See **www.musicalfutures.org.uk/ external+observers** for a leaflet developed by one of the Musical Futures pathfinder teachers, highlighting in detail what senior management/inspectors can expect to see in a typical Musical Futures lesson. It is also self-evident that you justify the reasons why you are following Musical Futures, what you hope to achieve for your students, and how it fits in with other provision you are offering in your music department.

MUSICAL FUTURES AND EXTERNAL OBSERVERS

students. Also, other students should be encouraged to model and demonstrate in the same way

- Music learning in school should be related to real-life musical tasks and made relevant to students

- Students are seen to be enjoying and achieving, and having positive attitudes towards their music lessons

- All students should be treated as musicians

- Students should develop a depth of musical response through skillfully exploring how music reflects its cultural context

- Audio recording should be used as an integral part of musical learning experiences

- Students should be learning from and through music, by integrating listening, composing and performing activities (rather than through being 'told about' music)

- Use of music technology and ICT should relate to the sorts of technologies students use outside school. ICT work should be related to its use in the 'real world', enabling students to explore and follow similar processes to those used professionally

- Students should have the opportunity to use their musical imagination and musical intelligence

- Musical vocabulary and notation should be used sensitively to reinforce the development of aural perception

- Music learning should focus on helping students discover the ways in which they learn best, and then help students apply their musical understanding across different musical experiences

It can therefore be expected that Ofsted will be looking for all of the above in a Musical Futures lesson, as in any other music lesson. Feedback from prior Musical Futures inspections indicates that they will also be looking for:

- Evidence of impact on extra-curricular activities, and ways in which schools are responding to different students needs (see the section on Extra-Curricular Provision, page 174, for ideas on how you might do this)

- Continuity of provision between Key Stages 2 and 3 (see the Whole Class Instrumental Work: Year 7 programme on page 76), and evidence of building on prior musical learning and experiences

- Continuity of provision, especially in teaching and learning styles, between Key Stages 3 and 4

- Evidence of tracking student progress through Musical Futures – which can be particularly effective through the use of ICT (for example NUMU, **www.numu.org.uk**)

- Good relationships between teachers and students, resulting in students working on task for the majority of the time

- Evidence of asking 'why' questions to students ('why have they chosen a particular song to copy', 'why do they think the bass line is difficult to play', 'why is the song structured in a particular way' etc) as this can help deepen understanding

- Impact of Musical Futures across the whole school

"Musical Futures is a good example of the long-term development of an initiative. While the progress of students is not always linear or obvious in every lesson, the real musical experience and the focus on the quality of re-creation enable students to make musical progress." (OFSTED)

CASE STUDY: FLEGG HIGH SCHOOL, NORFOLK

Fiona Sexton, head of performing arts at Flegg High School, Norfolk, describes her recent Ofsted music subject inspection, that was specifically looking at Musical Futures in practice

❝During our Ofsted subject inspection, I mentioned to the inspector that a true picture of the impact of Musical Futures on students' experiences in music lessons could only be gained with a long-term observation of their progress. However, Ofsted inspectors have to base their judgements on a snapshot view of every subject, meaning that prior preparation is vital so that the inspectors see the very best practice that Musical Futures can offer. Our preparation included all the normal planning and checking of documentation, but we put in place a few extra measures that were then highlighted as good Musical Futures practice.

I used our normal departmental scheme of work proforma to plan Musical Futures lessons, making sure I highlighted key points during every term for student feedback, evaluation and assessment. This structured approach on paper seemed to be appreciated, although I stressed to Ofsted that this was a set of guidelines rather than a prescriptive scheme. Monitoring and assessing students' progress was highlighted as an important issue and the inspector was particularly impressed with the way that we store work digitally as it means students can access recordings made in lesson time outside the music department.

A series of written sheets, with space for student and teacher feedback, meant that I was able to provide evidence of the quality of the work taking place. We use a lot of CD and DVD clips of professional bands and singers to provide our students with ideas and inspiration, and linking to 'real world' experience. This was highlighted as good practice, especially when it was linked to students assessing their own performances. The lesson that was particularly successful during the inspection was one that didn't actually contain students doing practical work but, instead, focused on them listening and evaluating their own and their peers performances.

We also had a lesson observed where the students were beginning the first project of the informal learning model (see page 130). The organisation of groups, recordings, lyrics, etc is a necessary part of the process but careful preparation is needed to avoid the impression of chaos. Setting up rooms or spaces with everything that a group will need prior to the lesson saves a lot of moving around; making sure that a CD and lyrics are available in case the students arrive without their stuff is also advisable. The inspector felt that, in this particular session, less meaningful learning had taken place than the previous session described above, but this was the beginning of a series of lessons rather than the end. It was fed-back that using students to model examples and provide feedback for each other should be included but not to 'over-evaluate'.

Like many music departments, the Musical Futures approach has given rise to an influx of students wanting rehearsal time away from normal music lessons. We have not yet put in place a robust system that monitors this so our evidence was only anecdotal, and we were criticised for not having enough students participating in music as an extra-curricular activity. This is difficult to monitor but is something that I would advise all music departments to consider. ❞

Flegg High School is a Musical Futures Champion School

SECTION 5
Appendices

Appendix 1: Evaluations

EVALUATION 1
Use this set of statements (or develop your own) before and after a Musical Futures programme, to assess whether your students' motivation, enjoyment and attitude of music has altered.

EVALUATION 2
Use and adapt this questionnaire at the end of each Musical Futures project, to enable students to reflect on their work, and consider how they might progress.

EVALUATION 1

Your name:

Your class:

How do you feel about the following aspects of your music? (5 = strongly agree; 1 = don't agree at all)

	1	2	3	4	5
I am confident in music lessons					
I enjoy music lessons					
I understand music					
I can play more than one instrument					
I have good musical skills					
I like singing					
I know about music technology					
I can play music in different styles					
I get involved in doing music, in and out of school					
I know where to go to get involved in the music I want					
I have met people into my kind of music					
Music lessons help me in other school subjects as well					
I am planning to take music at GCSE/BTEC/A level					
I know where to get help with my music when I need it					
I have the skills to make music with my friends, without needing the teacher's help					
I think I am musical					
I help others with learning music					
I enjoy listening to music					

EVALUATIONS

EVALUATION 2

Your name:

Your class:

1) How much did you enjoy the project?
(Please circle your answer)

- ○ Huge amount
- ○ It was good
- ○ It was ok
- ○ Some of it was ok
- ○ Didn't enjoy it

2) What did you/your group enjoy most about the project and why?

3) What did you/your group enjoy least about the project and why?

4) How did you feel about the role your teacher(s) took on during this project, and why?

5) How well do you feel you worked with other members of your group/class?

6) What, if anything, do you feel that you have learnt so far?

7) What would you like to do next with your music learning?

8) Anything else you would like to say about the project?

Appendix 2: Musical Futures Publications

The following are all available to download for free from **www.musicalfutures.org.uk**.

TEACHER RESOURCE PACK: FIRST EDITION

Practical suggestions and resources for implementing Musical Future, drawn from the pathfinder years of Musical Futures:

- *Personalising Music Learning: An Introduction*
- *The Whole Curriculum Approach*
- *Classroom Resources for Informal Music Learning at Key Stage 3*
- *Personalising Extra Curricular Activities for 11–18 Year Olds*

SUPPLEMENTARY PUBLICATIONS/PAMPHLETS

Guides for you and your school designed to help with Musical Futures:

- *Musical Futures and the Secondary National Strategy Key Stage 3 Programme*
- *Musical Futures and Special Educational Needs*
- *Music Department of the Future: Case study of new-build music department*
- *Personalising Music Learning in Your School: A Guide for Senior Managers*
- *An Emerging Vision – Shaping Music Education*
- *Personalising Music Learning*
- *Redefining Music Training*
- *Electrifying Music: A Guide to using ICT in Music Education*
- *Transforming Musical Leadership*
- *Supporting Young Musicians and Coordinating Musical Pathways*
- *From Vision to Practice: A Summary of Key Findings*
- *Simply CONNECT: Next Practice in Group Music Making and Musical Leadership*

Credits and Acknowledgements

Editor
Abigail D'Amore

Introduction/Implementing Musical Futures
Abigail D'Amore (Musical Futures) with Anna Gower (Monks Walk School), Ian Burton (Nottingham City Music Service) and David Price (Musical Futures)

Co-constructing a Curriculum
Ian Burton with Abigail D'Amore

Embedding Musical Futures
Abigail D'Amore, Martin Ainscough (Fred Longworth High School) and Anna Gower

Non-formal Teaching and Musical Futures
David Price

Guide to Classroom Workshopping
Tim Steiner (Guildhall CONNECT) with Robert Wells (Guildhall School of Music and Drama), David Price, and Abigail D'Amore

Filming: Jamie Quantrill (www.jpquantrill.com)

Participating Morpeth High School students:
Nancy Gray, Kalsuma Khanom, Luke Donovan, Kenny Mukendi, Yves Barbe-Wilson, An Tran, Chad Simpson, Ishan Alam, Heather Thomas, Samsul Rashid, Fahim Ali, Rebecca Gray, Grace Cybuch, Rayhan Khan, Vanessa Wilson, Aliya Alli

Whole Class Instrumental Work: Year 7
Ian Burton, Hannah Crawford, Claire Dyer (all Nottingham City Music Service), Andy Wolfe (Nottingham Emmanuel School)

Band Instrumental Work
Ian Burton with Sharon Jagdev Powell, Carolyn Davis and Helen Maltby (all Nottingham City Music Service)

Additional online materials: Martin Ainscough and Mark Flannery (www.showmehowtoplay.com)

Non-Western Music
Jonathan Kirby (Kagemusha Taiko) and Ian Burton with Sharon Jagdev Powell, Carolyn Davis and Helen Maltby

Guide to Songwriting
David Stoll (www.creativeconfidence.com)

Image Junction
Ian Burton with Sharon Jagdev Powell, Carolyn Davis and Helen Maltby

Case Study: Morpeth School
Peter Romhany (Morpeth School)

Informal Learning: Introduction/Implementing
Lucy Green (Institute of Education University of London) and Abigail D'Amore

In at the Deep End
Lucy Green and Abigail D'Amore

Modelling Aural Learning
Lucy Green and Abigail D'Amore
Additional online materials: Danny Fisher

Informal Composing
Lucy Green and Abigail D'Amore

Informal Learning with Other Musics
Lucy Green and Abigail D'Amore
Additional online materials: Danny Fisher and Abigail D'Amore

Case Study: Oasis Academy Lord's Hill
Paul Ibbott (Oasis Academy Lord's Hill)

Developing Extra-curricular Provision
Paul Kaiserman (Education Leeds Artforms) and David Price with Jo Richardson, Fiona Pacey, Fran Hannan, Abigail D'Amore and James Cross (High Storrs School)

Equipment and Music Technology
Abigail D'Amore, Anna Gower, Danny Fisher, Cliff Manning (NUMU), Sion Kemp (Roland UK) with Jenny Farn (Sheffield Park Academy) and Fran Hannan (Education Leeds Artforms)

Buildings, Space and Musical Futures
Abigail D'Amore, Anna Gower, Ian Sutton (Building Schools for the Future)

Musical Futures and External Observers
Abigail D'Amore and David Price with Fiona Sexton (Flegg High School)

ACKNOWLEDGEMENTS
These resource materials would not have been made possible without the invaluable support and contribution of all of those listed above and below.

We would like to thank the authors of the original teacher resource pack – particularly Lucy Green (Institute of Education) and Ian Burton (Nottingham City Music Service) – for their ongoing support of Musical Futures and their overwhelming contribution to this second edition. Also Anna Gower (Monks Walk School) for her invaluable advice and contribution. And of course David Price, whose continued leadership of Musical Futures has ensured that these materials reflect the changing nature of Musical Futures.

We are indebted to the staff and students from the following schools, who trialled and provided feedback on the new material of this resource pack:

- Peter Romhany and students from Morpeth School, Tower Hamlets
- Martin Ainscough and students from Fred Longworth High School, Wigan
- Jon Morgan and students from Northfleet Technology College, Kent
- Ian Tait and students from Banovallum School, Lincolnshire
- Anna Gower and students from Monks Walk School, Hertfordshire
- Emily Segal and students from Harrogate Grammar School, Harrogate

Also, staff and students from Monks Walk School, Hertfordshire; Morpeth School, Tower Hamlets; and Oasis Academy Lord's Hill, Southampton, for allowing photographs of their Musical Futures work to be used throughout these materials.

Aside from the above contributors the following have provided a valuable input: David Ashworth, Ann Barkway (Music Sales), David Barnard (Roland UK), Graham Bartholomew (Naxos), Sean Gregory (Guildhall CONNECT), Fran Hannan (Education Leeds Artforms), Jason Kubilius (Forest Hill School), Ocky Murray (Cog Design), Jo Richardson (Education Leeds Artforms), Adrian Scully (Synergy TV), Mark Taylor (Simon Balle School, Hertfordshire), Claire Turner (Cog Design), Catherine Walker (Music Sales), Joe Weiler (NUMU).

Finally grateful thanks to staff at the Paul Hamlyn Foundation for their contributions and support to the development and production of the materials, particularly Denise Barrows, Régis Cochefert, Robert Dufton, Dan Watson and Faye Williams.

Photography
© Emile Holba (www.emileholba.co.uk)

Design
Cog Design (www.cogdesign.com)

Print and distribution
Colourstream (www.colourstream.co.uk)

SECTION 5: APPENDICES